W9-DEF-759

Sarabeth's Good Morning Cookbook

Breakfast, Brunch, and Baking

Sarabeth Levine

with Genevieve Ko · Photographs by Quentin Bacon

New York Paris London Milan

For Bill

Your love and support have made our dreams and aspirations a reality—I always feel blessed that you are the first person I say "Good morning" to everyday.

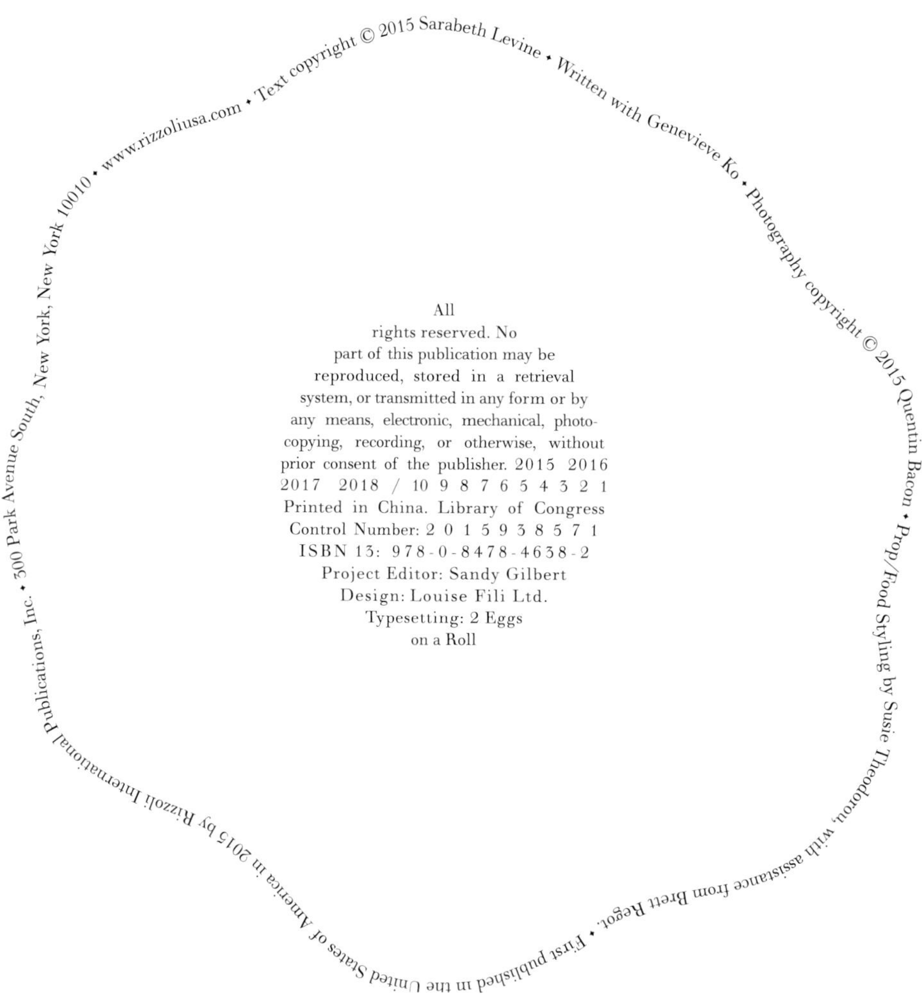

First published in the United States of America in 2015 by Rizzoli International Publications, Inc. • 300 Park Avenue South, New York, New York 10010 • www.rizzoliusa.com • Written with Genevieve Ko • Prop/Food Styling by Susie Theodorou, with assistance from Brett Regot.

 2015 2016 2017 2018 / 10 9 8 7 6 5 4 3 2 1 Printed in China. Library of Congress Control Number: 2 0 1 5 9 3 8 5 7 1 ISBN 13: 978-0-8478-4638-2 Project Editor: Sandy Gilbert Design: Louise Fili Ltd. Typesetting: 2 Eggs on a Roll

Contents

Introduction

I HAVE ALWAYS LOVED BREAKFAST. WHEN I WAS A CHILD, IT WAS MY FAVORITE MEAL OF THE DAY. IN FACT, EGGS AND FRENCH TOAST WERE THE EASY DISHES our mother prepared for us when she didn't have time to make a more traditional dinner. My love affair with breakfast has continued throughout the years and my morning recipes remain the foundation of the Sarabeth's restaurants.

In 1981, my husband Bill and I opened our first tiny shop on Amsterdam Avenue in New York City. Our plan was to have a place to produce and sell jams, which included my family's legendary orange-apricot marmalade. We also used the kitchen as a small bakery, where we made and served pastries, breads, and muffins to accompany the homemade jams. It seems like yesterday that we decided to start serving breakfast in that shop as well. And so, our journey began. For years people have come from far and wide to enjoy breakfast at Sarabeth's. It makes me happy to know that I have pleased so many customers for so long.

I'd like to continue bringing joy to others at the breakfast table with this book. It is filled with recipes to make weekday and weekend breakfasts special. You will find several of the signature dishes from our restaurants—and much more. I have included numerous recipes that I originally prepared in my home for friends and family. You will learn to make slow-cooked oatmeal like you have never tasted before, perfect omelets, fluffy pancakes, heavenly waffles, creamy quiches, quick jams, crisp potatoes, savory sides, and even soups and salads for brunch. There are also scrumptious baked goods from quick-and-easy scones and muffins to buttery coffee cakes and make-ahead yeasted breads. In addition to the recipes, I share tips and the techniques that I've refined over the years. These dishes will make your breakfasts memorable and your brunches unforgettable.

Good morning,

Sarabeth

Sarabeth's Pantry

THE BEAUTY OF BREAKFAST IS THAT YOU PROBABLY ALREADY HAVE EVERYTHING YOU NEED TO MAKE A COMPLETE MEAL. THROUGHOUT THE BOOK, I describe unique or special ingredients or tools required for specific chapters and recipes as needed. I don't want you to have to go out and track down hard-to-find ingredients or kitchen equipment to create breakfast and brunch at home. Feel free to work with whatever you have on hand. This is just a listing of widely used ingredients and tools for which I have preferences.

Flour: For all-purpose, I use unbleached and prefer King Arthur. For whole wheat, I like the fine grains of stone-ground.

Sugar: I usually use superfine because it dissolves more readily, making baked treats more tender and moist. If you can't find superfine sugar, pulse granulated sugar a few times in the food processor. If you're cooking sugar in spreads, you can use granulated, as it dissolves readily over direct heat.

Salt: For baking and some savory cooking, I use fine sea salt, which is finer and saltier than regular iodized salt. For other savory dishes, I use Diamond Crystal kosher salt. Because kosher salts vary in saltiness, if you use a different brand, season carefully to taste.

Butter: I always use Grade AA unsalted, which is sometimes labeled sweet butter. I use it both fresh and clarified (page 54), depending on the application.

Oil: For a neutral oil, I use canola. For olive oil, I use extra-virgin. I prefer milder, fruity ones, like Arbequina from Spain, for sweet baked goods, and more assertive ones from Italy for savory dishes, particularly those with other Italian flavors.

Dairy Products: Sour cream, cream cheese, and yogurt are full-fat unless otherwise specified. I call for whole milk when the recipe needs it; don't swap in lower-fat products when I list whole milk in the ingredients. Otherwise, you can use reduced- or low-fat milk, but not fat-free. Buttermilk is almost always sold low-fat. If you're lucky enough to find full-fat buttermilk, use it.

Eggs: Use Grade A large eggs. It doesn't matter whether the shells are brown or white.

Nuts and Seeds: Raw unsalted almonds, hazelnuts, pecans, pine nuts, peanuts, walnuts, sunflower seeds, and pumpkin seeds all make appearances here, and I prefer them toasted (page 41). Buy them whole and chop them yourself when needed.

Vanilla: I generally prefer to use vanilla beans for sauces, syrups, fruit spreads, and pastries. But vanilla beans are an indulgence, so I make the most of them by plumping them in alcohol. This not only extends their shelf life, it also enhances their deep floral flavor. The seeds also soften in the process, so you don't feel any grittiness wherever they're used.

Plumped Vanilla Beans

TO PLUMP VANILLA BEANS, CUT ⅛ INCH OFF THE BOTTOM OF EACH BEAN. STAND THE BEANS, CUT ENDS DOWN, IN A TALL GLASS JAR. POUR IN 2 INCHES OF DARK OR GOLDEN RUM. COVER the jar and let stand until the beans are softened, at least 2 weeks; they can be stored up to 2 months. To use a bean, simply run your thumb and index finger down the bean, or the length of bean you'd like to use, to release the seeds. If using the pod, split it lengthwise to release more flavor. When a recipe calls for less than a whole bean, return the unused part to the jar. You can substitute vanilla extract in some recipes, as long as you use pure extract, not imitation.

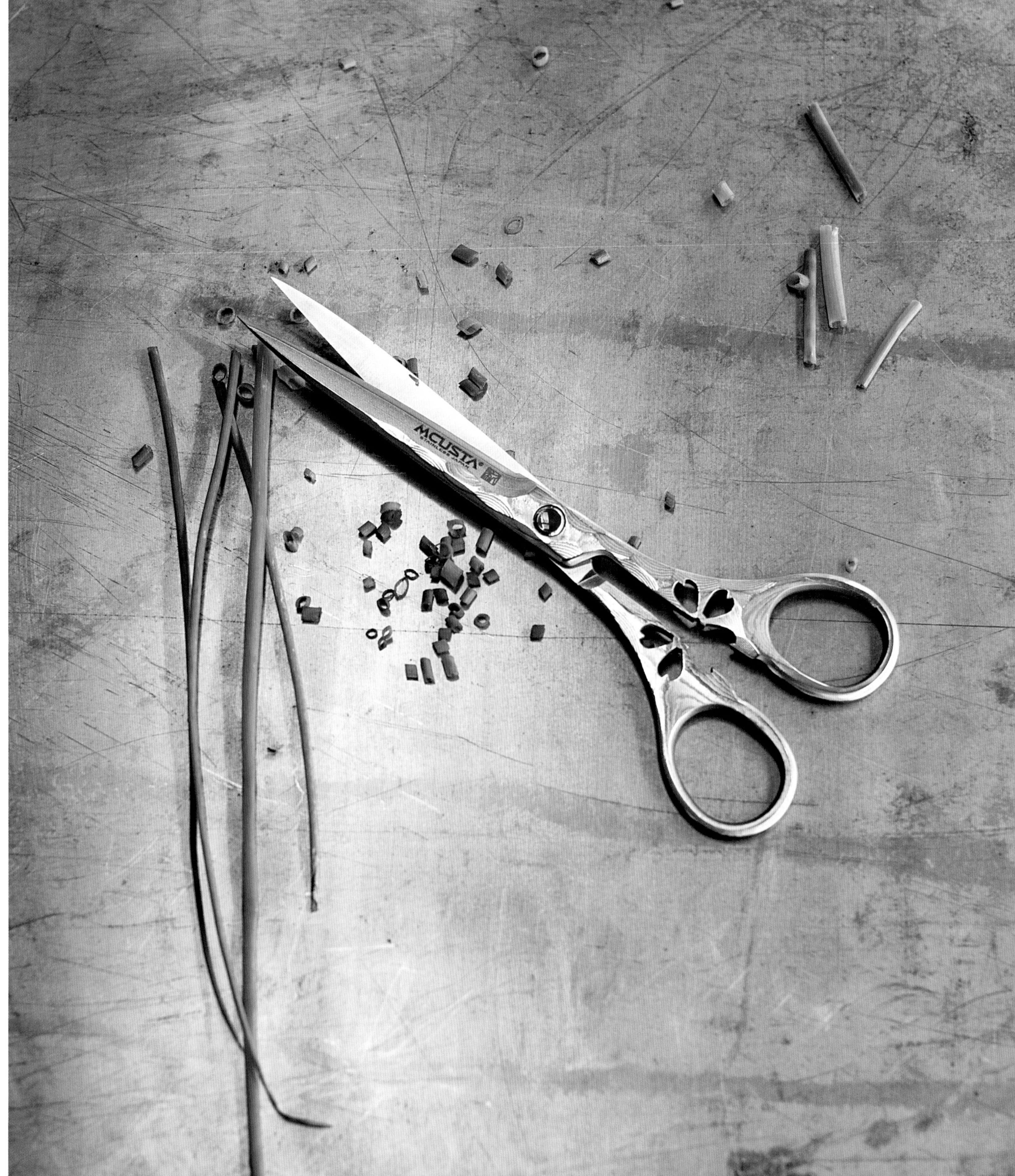
MCUSTA

SARABETH'S GO-TO TOOLS

Dry Measuring Cups and Spoons: I use a set of professional measuring cups and spoons that are heavy and sturdy. They're pricey but worth the investment, as they don't dent or warp and the handles stay straight. I highly recommend either buying professional sets or using a kitchen scale for measuring.

Liquid Measuring Cups: I rely on my measuring cups not only for measuring liquids, but also for controlling the pouring of wet ingredients from their spouts. In some cases, I even save myself the trouble of washing an extra bowl by mixing directly in the cup. I prefer sturdy glass cups with clear markings.

Kitchen Scale: For this book, I tested all of the recipes measuring ingredients by both weight and volume. Weight is the more reliable and uniform method. Look for digital scales with easy-to-read numerical readouts and a full range of increments from ¼ ounce to 11 pounds or so. However, because most scales for home cooks can be imprecise when it comes to measuring small amounts of lightweight ingredients, I have provided the weights only for measurements of ¼ cup and above. The exception is for yeast since compressed yeast is easier to measure on a scale and active dry yeast can be purchased in packets by weight.

Parchment Paper: Parchment paper prevents items from sticking during cooking or baking, makes for easy cleanup, and is in constant use in my kitchen.

Bench Scraper: Also known as a bench knife or dough scraper, this tool has a thin, flat, rectangular metal blade with a handle. I use it to cut dough and butter and scrape work surfaces clean with a single swipe. Be careful if using this tool on stone surfaces, as it may scratch them.

Silicone Spatulas: I'm always reaching for these heatproof spatulas to stir or spread mixtures and scrape bowls clean.

Whisks: Once you try a professional-grade whisk with sturdy wires like the one I use, you may never go back to a flimsy regular one.

Half-Sheet Pans: These are the most useful all-purpose pans for sweet baking and savory cooking. They also come in handy for holding and transporting ingredients and dishes in the kitchen. The pans measure 13 inches long, 8 inches wide, and 1 inch deep. Be sure to buy commercial-quality pans made of heavy-gauge aluminum, which are now readily available in most housewares stores.

Electric Appliances: I rely on a few kitchen appliances to make cooking and baking breakfast recipes a breeze. I regularly use a heavy-duty stand mixer, handheld electric mixer, immersion (stick) blender, food processor, and blender.

CUPS
2
500
400
14
12
10
8

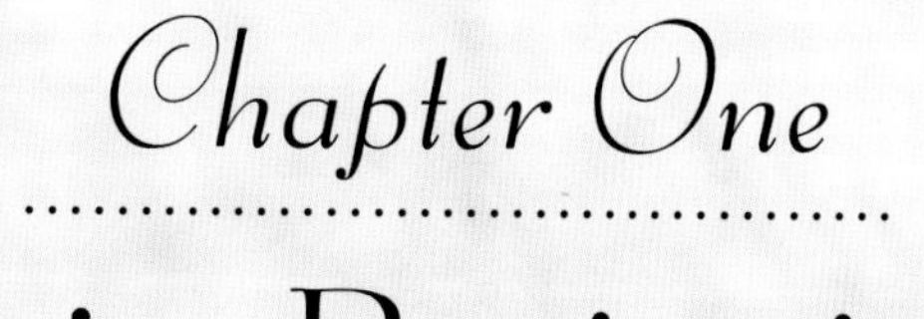

Chapter One

Fruity Beginnings

MANY MORNINGS, I START MY DAY SIMPLY WITH A PIECE OF FRESH FRUIT. THERE ARE FEW THINGS THAT MAKE ME HAPPIER THAN BITING into ripe, juicy fruit. On workdays, I often dart across the hall of my flagship bakery in New York City's Chelsea Market to buy some at the fruit grocer. On summer weekends, I stop by the farm stands near my home on Long Island and purchase just-picked produce directly from the farmers.

When I don't have perfect fruit—and even when I do—I sometimes choose to cook it. My poached apples and pears are the ultimate fall comfort and my stone fruit compote captures the sweetness of summer. Other times, I drink my fruit in the form of smoothies, juices, or even cocktails. Breakfast isn't complete without a bit of beautiful fruit, and when you make the recipes here, you'll turn even a quick daily meal into a stunning, satisfying one.

KEY INGREDIENTS

Preparing fresh fruits is easy; choosing the best ones is tougher. I prefer organic, seasonal fruit from local farms. If the fruit isn't quite ripe, I let it ripen on my kitchen windowsill. To figure out when the fruit is ripe, I give it a sniff to see if it's fragrant and a little squeeze to feel if it's yielding.

TOOL KIT

All you really need to prepare fruit is a very sharp knife, a vegetable peeler, and a good cutting board. Since I opened my bakeries and restaurants in Japan, I've relied on knives I buy there. You don't need to cross the Pacific to get a high-quality knife, but I do recommend Japanese knives because of their thin, sharp blades. They slice cleanly through even the softest, most delicate fruit. Just be sure to sharpen the blade regularly.

For fruit drinks, you need a blender. While a powerful commercial brand will make blending large quantities into smooth drinks fast and easy, smaller home models work just as well. If you can't fit everything into the pitcher without overfilling it, simply blend in batches.

Citrus Sundial

Makes 1 serving

Like the Morning Fruit Bowl (page 10), this dish revolves around the presentation. Any citrus works well here, but you can experiment with unique varieties for bursts of color. The tangy, juicy fruit becomes a morning meal when paired with creamy refreshing yogurt and crunchy granola. To make these for a big brunch party, compose the sundials ahead of time and refrigerate. Then simply dollop on the toppings just before serving.

1 grapefruit
1 navel orange
¼ cup (65 grams) plain yogurt
2 tablespoons Morning Crunch Granola (page 38)
Honey or pure maple syrup, for drizzling, optional

1 With a sharp knife, trim off the top and bottom of the grapefruit. Stand the grapefruit upright on a cutting board and slice off the peel and pith in sections, using a sawing motion and working from top to bottom around the fruit. Cut between the membranes to release the grapefruit segments. Repeat with the orange. On a serving plate, alternate the segments to create a "sundial" pattern.

2 Dollop the yogurt in the center of the fruit and sprinkle the granola on top. If desired, drizzle with honey.

Morning Fruit Bowl

Makes 1 serving

At our first restaurant, I'd take a daily midmorning break, make myself a beautiful bowl of cut fruit, and sit down to enjoy it. It wasn't anything fancy, but customers would peer over at my table and tell their servers, "I'll have what she's having." That was the birth of my signature Sarabeth's Fruit Bowl on our menus. To this day, fresh fruit is what so many people crave first thing in the morning. I love fruit and will snack on it straight, but presenting it attractively makes it that much more delicious.

1 small pink grapefruit
1 navel orange
1 banana
4 strawberries

1 With a sharp knife, trim off the top and bottom of the grapefruit. Stand the grapefruit upright on a cutting board and slice off the peel and pith in sections, using a sawing motion and working from top to bottom around the fruit. Cut between the membranes to release the grapefruit segments and arrange the segments in the center of a serving bowl. Repeat with the orange. Gently toss with the grapefruit.

2 Peel and slice the banana and fan around the citrus mixture. Hull and slice the strawberries and arrange in the center of the bowl. Or, gently combine the bananas and strawberries with the citrus segments.

Poached "Baked" Apples in Ginger Ale and Maple Syrup

Makes 4 servings

Many years ago, my mother's uncle owned the Tip Toe Inn, a family-style restaurant on the Upper West Side of Manhattan. Poached apples were one of the most popular items on the menu, and the dish deserves a comeback here. My family found that gently poaching the apples in ginger ale rendered them tender, juicy, and flavorful. I've kept that tradition, as well as that of serving the apples with a pitcher of heavy cream. But I've also updated the original: I added maple syrup and vanilla simply because I adore both flavors. Though I still often poach Rome Beauty apples, as my family used to, I sometimes swap in smaller apples such as Jonagolds. I look for fruit with a meaty texture that will hold its shape while cooking and a deep scarlet color for a stunning presentation.

4 large Rome Beauty apples (about 12 ounces; 340 grams each) or 6 smaller apples (about 9 ounces; 255 grams each)

4 cups (896 grams) ginger ale

2 cups (448 grams) unsweetened apple juice

½ cup (98 grams) packed light brown sugar

⅓ cup (97 grams) pure maple syrup

1 vanilla bean, preferably a Plumped Vanilla Bean (page 3)

1 cinnamon stick

2 cups (464 grams) heavy cream, for serving

1 Using a vegetable peeler, remove a ½-inch-wide strip of peel from the top of each apple. Using an apple corer, core each apple three-quarters of the way down to the bottom—be careful not to go through the bottom of the apple. Using a paring knife, remove any remaining skin around the cored area. In a nonreactive 7-quart Dutch oven or other heavy pot, arrange the apples cored sides up in a single layer.

2 In a large bowl, mix the ginger ale, apple juice, brown sugar, and maple syrup. Using the tip of a knife, split the vanilla bean and scrape the seeds into the liquid (or, if using a plumped vanilla bean, squeeze out the seeds); reserve the pod. Pour the mixture over the apples, letting it fill the cored centers. The liquid should come two-thirds up the sides (and insides) of the apples. If necessary, add water. Add the cinnamon stick and the reserved vanilla pod.

3 Bring the liquid to a boil over medium-high heat. Reduce the heat to low, cover, and simmer for 10 minutes. Turn the apples over, cover, and cook for 10 minutes. Turn the apples right side up, cover again, and simmer just until the apples are tender when pierced with the tip of a small sharp knife, about 5 more minutes. Using a slotted spoon, transfer the apples to a deep plate to cool.

4 Meanwhile, bring the cooking liquid to a boil over high heat and cook, uncovered, until syrupy and reduced to about 2 cups, about 25 minutes. Remove and discard the cinnamon stick and vanilla pod. Cool the syrup completely.

5 Pour the cooled syrup over the apples. Cover with plastic wrap and refrigerate until chilled, at least 2 hours, or up to overnight.

6 To serve, place the apples in dishes and pour the cooking syrup around them. Serve with the cream.

Peach and Plum Compote

Makes 6 servings

When I was a child, I loved my mother's treats. She was a working mom, which was unusual in those days, so her signature recipe consisted of opening a can of peaches and a can of plums. She'd pour them, with their syrup, into a Tupperware container and refrigerate the magenta mix. All week long, she'd dole out servings with generous spoonfuls of sour cream. I've captured that childhood memory in this fresh version. Maple syrup and vanilla bean seeds add a nice dimension, but it's summer fruit that shines here. Although you should use the best you can find, even less tasty fruit becomes succulent in this syrup. Sour cream is still my preferred accompaniment, but Whipped Cream (page 50)—or even ice cream—tastes great with the chilled compote. Sometimes I also ladle it warm over waffles or pancakes.

1½ cups (336 grams) unsweetened apple juice

¾ cup (219 grams) pure maple syrup

3 tablespoons fresh lemon juice

4 slightly firm ripe peaches (about 6 ounces; 170 grams each), peeled, pitted, and quartered

4 slightly firm ripe red plums (about 4 ounces; 114 grams each), halved and pitted

Seeds from ½ vanilla bean, preferably a Plumped Vanilla Bean (page 3), or ½ teaspoon pure vanilla extract

1 In a nonreactive 5-quart Dutch oven or other heavy pot, mix the apple juice, maple syrup, and lemon juice. Add the peaches and plums and bring to a simmer over medium-high heat. Reduce the heat to low, cover, and simmer until the fruit is barely tender, about 15 minutes.

2 Remove the Dutch oven from the heat and stir in the vanilla seeds. Let stand until slightly cooled, or cool completely, cover, and refrigerate for up to 3 days. Serve warm or chilled.

Pear, Ginger, and Yogurt Parfaits

Makes 4 servings

For an elegant fruit dish for a brunch, you couldn't do much better than these parfaits. They can look chic and slim in fluted champagne glasses or hip and homey in Mason jars. I prefer the invigorating tang of thick goat's-milk yogurt, which is now readily available in supermarkets, but there are so many varieties of luscious, creamy yogurt in the refrigerated cases that you should use the one you like best. Be sure to use plain yogurt, though (the more fat the tastier), as the poached pears bring plenty of sweetness.

½ cup (98 grams) granulated sugar

¾ cup (168 grams) water

1 tablespoon fresh lemon juice

½ vanilla bean, preferably a Plumped Vanilla Bean (page 3)

4 firm, almost ripe d'Anjou pears (about 11 ounces; 312 grams each), peeled, cored, and cut into ½-inch cubes

1 cup (261 grams) plain yogurt

3 tablespoons finely chopped crystallized ginger

4 small fresh mint sprigs

1 In a wide saucepan or skillet just large enough to hold the cubed pears in a single layer, bring the sugar, water, and lemon juice to a boil over high heat, stirring to dissolve the sugar. Reduce the heat to low, cover, and simmer for 5 minutes.

2 Using the tip of a knife, split the half vanilla bean and scrape the seeds into the mixture (or, if using a plumped vanilla bean, squeeze out the seeds); add the pod. Stir to distribute the seeds evenly. Add the pears and bring to a boil over medium heat. Reduce the heat to low, cover, and simmer, stirring occasionally, until the pears are just tender, about 10 minutes. Using a slotted spoon, carefully transfer the pears to a medium bowl.

3 Bring the syrup to a boil and cook until reduced by one-third, about 3 minutes. Let cool.

4 Pour the syrup over the pears. Cover tightly with plastic wrap and refrigerate until chilled, at least 2 hours, or up to overnight.

5 To serve, divide half of the pears, with a bit of the syrup, among four glasses. Top with half of the yogurt, then half of the ginger. Top with the remaining pears, yogurt, and ginger. Garnish with the mint sprigs. Reserve the remaining pear syrup, with the vanilla bean, for another use; it can be refrigerated in an airtight container for up to 1 week.

Banana-Strawberry Smoothie

Makes 1 to 2 servings (about 2½ cups)

I believe a great smoothie has to be thick. That's why I always add a banana and ice cubes to the mix. The luscious texture makes it feel as decadent as a special treat even though it's healthy. When the fruit needs more oomph, I blend in a touch of jam to echo its natural sweetness. For a rich and creamy dairy-free smoothie, be sure to try the variation below.

1 large banana (about 4½ ounces; 127 grams)

6 medium strawberries (about 4½ ounces; 127 grams), hulled

½ cup (117 grams) plain Greek yogurt

½ cup (112 grams) 2% reduced-fat milk

Seeds from ¼ vanilla bean, preferably a Plumped Vanilla Bean (page 3), or ¼ teaspoon pure vanilla extract

3 large ice cubes

1 to 2 teaspoons strawberry jam, preferably homemade (page 178), or to taste, optional

1 In a blender, puree the banana and strawberries with the yogurt, milk, vanilla seeds, and ice until smooth.

2 Taste and add the jam, if desired. Blend again and drink immediately.

Almond Milk Nectarine-Raspberry Smoothie: Substitute 1 cup (6 ounces; 170 grams) raspberries and 1 large nectarine (5 ounces; 142 grams), pitted and chopped, for the strawberries. Substitute ½ cup (112 grams) almond milk for the yogurt and milk, and pure maple syrup for the optional jam.

Vanilla Bean Lemonade

Makes 6 to 8 servings (about 9 cups)

This not-too-sweet lemonade is bracing and perfect with food. The vanilla bean seeds add a unique aromatic twist. Undissolved sugar is the enemy of lemonade, so I always start with a simple syrup. To get the most juice from your lemons, they must be at room temperature. To add a little caffeine kick, stir in iced tea as directed in the Arnold Palmer below. For another type of kick, try the hard lemonade version.

1 cup (200 grams) granulated sugar

7 cups (1.6 kilograms) water

1¾ cups (392 grams) fresh lemon juice

Seeds from 1 vanilla bean, preferably a Plumped Vanilla Bean (page 3)

1 In a small saucepan, bring the sugar and 1 cup (224 grams) water to a boil over high heat, stirring to dissolve the sugar. Reduce the heat to medium and boil for 5 minutes. Cool completely.

2 In a large pitcher, stir together the cooled syrup, lemon juice, vanilla seeds, and the remaining 6 cups (1.3 kilograms) water. Cover and refrigerate until chilled, at least 2 hours, or up to overnight. Serve chilled.

Arnold Palmer: In step 2, substitute 6 cups (1.3 kilograms) chilled unsweetened iced tea for the water.

Hard Lemonade: Stir citrus or regular vodka into the lemonade. Use as much or as little as you'd like—the vodka doesn't add flavor, so the amount is up to you.

Crunchy No-Booze Bloody Mary

Makes 8 servings (about 6 cups)

The pickled vegetables make this drink. They not only crown the glass for an impressive presentation, but they also infuse the drink itself. Their tart crunch turns this standard into a great wake-me-up. You can even transform the Bloody Mary into a savory appetizer by topping it with crabmeat or hooking a jumbo cooked shrimp on the glass. Whether you're serving this as a drink or a dish, you'll want to pass out forks for guests to spear the pickles.

5¾ cups (46 ounces; 1.3 kilograms) tomato juice

⅓ cup (75 grams) fresh lemon juice

2 tablespoons fresh lime juice

¼ cup (56 grams) Worcestershire sauce

2 tablespoons grated fresh or drained prepared horseradish

20 drops Tabasco sauce

1 cup (112 grams) Bloody Mary Pickles (page 183), plus more for garnish

Freshly ground black pepper

1 In a large pitcher, stir together the tomato juice, lemon juice, lime juice, Worcestershire sauce, horseradish, and Tabasco sauce. Cover and refrigerate until very cold, at least 2 hours, or up to 2 days.

2 Place 2 tablespoons of the pickles in each of eight ice-filled tall glasses. Stir the drink mixture and divide it among the glasses. Grind a little black pepper on top of each, then garnish with more pickles.

Boozy Bloody Mary: Add 1 to 2 ounces (28 to 56 grams) vodka to each glass before serving.

Four Flowers Juice

Makes 8 to 10 servings (about 11 cups)

We've been serving this sunset-hued juice since the day we opened our first restaurant. I was inspired by a four flowers sorbet I tasted at French chef Georges Blanc's Michelin-starred restaurant. Instead of his floral flavors, I went in a very fruity direction. This no-fail formula has become the signature drink at Sarabeth's.

6 tablespoons (74 grams) granulated sugar
2 cups plus 6 tablespoons (532 grams) water
1 pound (454 grams) fresh pineapple chunks
3 large bananas (about 4½ ounces; 127 grams each), peeled and quartered
4 cups (896 grams) fresh orange juice
2 tablespoons fresh lemon juice
1 tablespoon grenadine

1 In a small saucepan, combine the sugar and 6 tablespoons water and bring to a boil, stirring to dissolve the sugar. Remove the syrup from the heat and cool completely.

2 In a blender or food processor, puree the pineapple and bananas until very smooth. Working in batches if necessary, add the orange juice, lemon juice, grenadine, syrup, and the remaining 2 cups (448 grams) water and puree until very smooth. If you prefer a thinner juice, strain through a sieve.

3 Transfer to a pitcher, cover, and refrigerate until very cold, at least 2 hours, or up to 2 days.

4 Divide the juice among glasses and serve.

Four Flowers Mimosa: Fill champagne flutes one-third full with Four Flowers Juice. Top off with a slightly dry Prosecco or cava. Serve immediately.

Chapter Two
Whole Grains

I'M A GRAIN GIRL. THE RANGE OF FLAVORS THAT DIFFERENT WHOLE GRAINS OFFER IS SPECTACULAR, BUT THEIR TEXTURES ARE WHAT REALLY GET ME. I like grains creamy in porridge and milk toasts; crunchy in granola, crackers, and cookies; or chewy in bars and bread. Perhaps what I love most about grains is that they're an everyday breakfast, as appropriate for on-the-go mornings as for seated weekend brunches.

Although I cook hot cereal low and slow, I throw together my milk toasts in minutes. Baked goods take some time, but once you have them on hand, they're ready any day of the week. A simple serving of delicious whole grains in the morning will energize you for the day ahead.

KEY INGREDIENTS

Whole Grains: There is such a thing as fresh grains. If you happen to live near a mill, buy freshly milled oats and other grains. Some producers around the country are returning to heirloom varieties that have more complex flavors. Nowadays we're lucky enough to have a full range of whole grains in regular supermarkets. I prefer organic and always look for the latest "best by" date before choosing a package. If I'm not going to use the grains right away, I store them in airtight containers in the freezer to prevent them from going rancid.

Sweeteners: Give a flavor boost to any bowl of cereal with granular golden sugars such as Demerara, turbinado, maple, or coconut; liquid sweeteners, including aromatic honeys, maple syrup, and sorghum; and fruity preserves, syrups, butters, and jams (pages 165 to 181).

Dairy: Cereal is nothing without milk. Skim or low-fat milk, soy, or almond milk may be a way of life for many of us, but cereal with whole milk can make an eye-opening difference. For the ultimate indulgence, use a little splash of half-and-half. When serving hot cereal, warm the milk so the cereal doesn't cool down quickly. Yogurt and granola go hand in hand. Buy plain yogurt and sweeten it to your taste. Full-fat varieties taste best, but lower-fat options work fine.

Fruit: Fresh fruit is always a welcome addition to morning cereal. Sliced strawberries and bananas are the most popular, but consider raspberries, blueberries, apricots, peaches, plums, or even mangoes—the possibilities are endless. Dried fruit works well any time of year, but especially in winter. In addition to classic raisins, try dried cranberries, blueberries, strawberries, cherries, or coarsely chopped dried apples, which are especially good in hot cereal. If you really want to give your cereal a wake-up call, sprinkle it with minced crystallized ginger (also wonderful with dried apricots) or chopped dates (which are so sweet you'll probably skip the sugar).

Nuts and Seeds: All nuts and seeds echo the nutty flavor and crunch of whole grains. Buy the best and freshest you can find. Get them raw and unsalted so that you can toast them yourself (page 41). If you're not using them right away, store them in airtight containers in the freezer.

TOOL KIT

Double Boiler: I use a double boiler to cook all cereal grains into hot porridge. It may take a little longer, but the results are absolutely worthwhile: The cereals end up incomparably creamy and delicious. If you don't have a double boiler, you can fashion your own: Choose a metal bowl that will fit snugly on top of a saucepan. Glass and ceramic bowls may crack over boiling water; do not use them. Fill the saucepan with enough water to simmer for a long period of time, keeping in mind that the water should not touch the bottom of the bowl. You can cover the bowl with either a lid or foil. Be sure to use oven mitts or a kitchen towel when handling the bowl, as it will get hot.

Ramekins: Hot Cereal Soufflés (page 35) are baked in 6-ounce ceramic ramekins or ovenproof glass dishes. The straight sides help them rise.

Old-Fashioned Oatmeal

Makes 4 servings

With so many instant varieties on the market, the skill of slowly cooking rolled oats is vanishing. But pasty, overcooked oatmeal is not for me, and I'm willing to wait for a perfect bowl of oatmeal. The key to capturing oats' earthy flavor is gentle cooking in a double boiler and not stirring, which can create a starchy wallpaper-paste texture. My method yields a wheaty taste and well-plumped grains that retain a bit of crunch. Be sure to eat the oatmeal right away—you can't let it sit. But that last part is easy. You won't be able to resist digging into the steaming bowl.

COOK'S NOTE: Buy old-fashioned rolled oats, which are whole oat grains that have been flattened between rollers. Quick-cooking oatmeal is the same thing, but the grains are pressed flatter so they cook more quickly; instant oatmeal is flatter still. I like really thick oats—the thicker the better. They may take a bit longer to cook, but they're worth the extra minutes.

2 cups (206 grams) old-fashioned rolled oats
4 cups (896 grams) cold water
¼ teaspoon fine sea salt
Warm milk, for serving
Sugar, pure maple syrup, or honey, for serving

1 In the top of a double boiler, mix the oats, water, and salt. Place over cold water in the bottom of the double boiler and cover. (Alternatively, mix the oats, water, and salt in a medium metal bowl and set over cold water in a saucepan that holds the bowl snugly. The water should not touch the bottom of the bowl. Cover the bowl with foil or a lid.) Bring the water to a boil over medium heat. Reduce the heat to low to maintain a steady yet gentle simmer and cook, without stirring, until the oatmeal is plump and tender, about 30 minutes.

2 Remove from the heat and let stand, still covered, for 5 minutes. Stir the oatmeal gently. Serve immediately, with warm milk and the sweetener of your choice.

Slow-Cooked Steel-Cut Oats

Makes 4 servings

Oh my god, the crunch. It's the crunch that I love in this cereal, along with that very strong, very earthy oat flavor. But even though I enjoy that crisp-chewy texture, I'm very careful to cook steel-cut oats all the way through. For years, I've used McCann's Steel Cut Irish Oatmeal, which is made from the finest steel-cut oats. Nowadays, there are lots of options available at the market. Try them all and choose the one you like best.

1 cup (187 grams) steel-cut oats
4 cups (896 grams) cold water
¼ teaspoon fine sea salt
Warm milk, for serving
2 medium bananas, sliced

1 In the top of a double boiler, mix the oats, water, and salt. Place over cold water in the bottom of the double boiler and cover. (Alternatively, mix the oats, water, and salt in a medium metal bowl and set over cold water in a saucepan that holds the bowl snugly. The water should not touch the bottom of the bowl. Cover the bowl with foil or a lid.) Bring the water to a boil over medium heat. Reduce the heat to low to maintain a steady yet gentle simmer and cook, stirring once or twice, until the oatmeal is plump and tender, about 50 minutes.

2 Remove from the heat and let stand, still covered, for 5 minutes. Stir the oatmeal gently. Serve immediately, with warm milk and sliced bananas.

Five-Grain Hot Cereal

Makes 4 servings

Once, years ago, I purchased Old Wessex Ltd. 5 Grain Cereal from the organic section of the supermarket. What a surprise! With a blend of whole oats, rye, triticale, barley, and flaxseed, it's extremely healthy, but it really became my go-to favorite because I like getting a variety of flavors all in one spoonful. Since then, I've tried other brands, such as Bob's Red Mill, which is also fabulous. This is especially nice on cold winter mornings.

1 cup (112 grams) 5-grain cereal
2½ cups (560 grams) cold water
¼ teaspoon fine sea salt
Warm milk, for serving
Coarsely chopped dried mangoes, for serving
Coarsely chopped roasted cashews, for serving
Maple sugar, for serving

1 In the top of a double boiler, mix the cereal, water, and salt. Place over cold water in the bottom of the double boiler and cover. (Alternatively, mix the cereal, salt, and water in a medium metal bowl and set over cold water in a saucepan that holds the bowl snugly. The water should not touch the bottom of the bowl. Cover the bowl with foil or a lid.) Bring the water to a boil over medium heat. Reduce the heat to low so the water maintains a steady yet gentle simmer. Cook, covered, stirring once or twice, until the grains are plump and tender, about 25 minutes.

2 Remove from the heat and let stand, still covered, for 5 minutes. Stir the cereal gently. Serve immediately, with warm milk, mangoes, cashews, and maple sugar.

Six-Grain Hot Cereal: Substitute fresh red and golden raspberries and a spoonful of Cooked Wheat Berries (page 32) for the mangoes and cashews (photo opposite).

Top to Taste

PERFECTLY COOKED OATMEAL CAN BE A COMPLETE, SATISFYING MEAL ON ITS OWN, BUT A LITTLE SWEETENER AND WARM MILK MAKE IT LUXURIOUS, AND ADDITIONAL SEASONINGS take it over the top. Add whatever you'd like to your oatmeal. Be creative with what's in your pantry, pairing flavors you love. These are just a few of my favorite combinations:

Top oatmeal with raisins and a sliced banana and sweeten with honey. If desired, garnish with a single perfect strawberry dipped in honey.

Sprinkle some Cooked Wheat Berries (below) over oatmeal. Top with a pat of unsalted butter, then sliced bananas. Sweeten with light brown sugar.

Cooked Wheat Berries

WHEAT BERRIES ARE WHOLE WHEAT KERNELS FROM COMMON WHEAT, INCLUDING THE BRAN, GERM, AND ENDOSPERM. THEY CAN BE FOUND IN SUPERMARKETS AND NATURAL food stores. They add a gentle crunch to cereals, pancake batters, and breads and taste great sprinkled on salads.

To cook wheat berries, rinse ½ cup (50 grams) wheat berries under cold running water and drain. Place in a medium saucepan and add cold water to cover by 1 inch. Bring to a boil over high heat. Cover, reduce the heat to low, and simmer until the wheat berries are barely tender (they should retain a little chewiness), about 1 hour or longer, depending on their age. If all the water is absorbed before the berries are tender, add more. Drain in a colander, rinse under cold water, and drain. The cooked wheat berries can be refrigerated in an airtight container for up to 3 days. Makes about 1½ cups.

Creamy Wheat Cereal

Makes 4 servings

One of my favorite childhood breakfasts seems to have fallen out of favor and I'm not sure why. Wheatena has an intense wheat flavor with a hint of the earthy richness you find in fresh grains. And the tiny grains become almost silky when cooked. I prepare it with a lot of milk to draw out its natural sweetness. Because I so closely associate a steaming bowl of this hot cereal with cold winter mornings, I like to stir in dried cranberries and blueberries and drizzle maple syrup on top.

2 cups (448 grams) cold milk
2 cups (448 grams) cold water
1⅓ cups (177 grams) wheat cereal, such as Wheatena
½ cup (92 grams) dried blueberries
½ cup (80 grams) dried cranberries
2 teaspoons unsalted butter
¼ teaspoon fine sea salt
Pure maple syrup or maple sugar, for serving
Half-and-half, light cream, or milk, for serving

1 In the top of a double boiler, mix the milk, water, cereal, blueberries, cranberries, butter, and salt. Place over cold water in the bottom of the double boiler. (Alternatively, mix the milk, water, cereal, blueberries, cranberries, butter, and salt in a large metal bowl and set over cold water in a saucepan that holds the bowl snugly. The water should not touch the bottom of the bowl.) Bring the water to a boil over medium heat. Reduce the heat to low to maintain a steady yet gentle simmer and cook, uncovered, stirring frequently, until the cereal is tender and the liquid is absorbed, about 20 minutes.

2 Serve immediately, with maple syrup and half-and-half.

Hot Cereal Soufflés

Makes 4 servings

What an elegant way to serve breakfast! The simple addition of egg yolks and beaten whites to your favorite cereal can transform it into something really special. A spoonful of jam in the bottom of the ramekin provides an instant sauce for your soufflé.

Softened unsalted butter, for the ramekins

½ cup (157 grams) Mandarin Orange Spread (page 176)

2½ cups (560 grams) whole milk

¾ cup (132 grams) farina or wheat cereal, such as Cream of Wheat

3 large eggs, separated, at room temperature

1 tablespoon unsalted butter

1 tablespoon superfine sugar

Seeds from ½ vanilla bean, preferably a Plumped Vanilla Bean (page 3), or ½ teaspoon pure vanilla extract

¼ teaspoon fine sea salt

Heavy cream or half-and-half, for serving

1 Position a rack in the center of the oven and preheat to 400°F. Lightly brush the insides of four 6-ounce ramekins or ovenproof glass dishes with softened butter. Spoon 2 tablespoons jam into each ramekin.

2 In the top of a double boiler, whisk the milk and farina. Place over cold water in the bottom of the double boiler. (Alternatively, whisk the milk and farina in a medium metal bowl and set over cold water in a saucepan that holds the bowl snugly. The water should not touch the bottom of the bowl.) Bring the water to a boil over medium heat. Reduce the heat to low to maintain a steady yet gentle simmer and cook, uncovered, stirring frequently, until the cereal is tender and the liquid is absorbed, about 15 minutes. Remove the top from the bottom pot.

3 In a large bowl, beat the egg yolks. Gradually stir in the hot cereal, then stir in the butter, sugar, vanilla seeds, and salt.

4 In a clean medium bowl, using a clean whisk, beat the egg whites with a handheld electric mixer on high speed until soft peaks form. Add one-quarter of the whites to the cereal mixture and stir with a silicone spatula to lighten. Add the remaining whites and fold in until just combined.

5 Divide the cereal mixture among the prepared ramekins and gently smooth the tops. Place the ramekins on a half-sheet pan. Bake until the soufflés are puffed and lightly browned, about 15 minutes.

6 Serve immediately. Instruct your guests to deflate the soufflés by making holes in the centers with spoons and then to pour a bit of cream into the holes.

Creamy Polenta
with Peaches and Chestnut Honey

Makes 4 to 6 servings

In many parts of the country, white corn grits are everyday breakfast fare. This polenta recipe is my nod to grits. Polenta is essentially the same as grits, but with the golden hue of yellow cornmeal. It can be served as a savory dish or a sweet one, and here I've chosen to go with the latter. Ripe peaches and honey give a juicy boost of flavor. Be sure to cook the polenta slowly while whisking frequently to ensure that it is very tender.

4 cups (896 grams) cold water
¾ teaspoon fine sea salt
1 cup (160 grams) polenta (coarse yellow cornmeal)
1 tablespoon unsalted butter
Ripe peaches, sliced, for serving
Chestnut honey, for serving

1 In a heavy-bottomed medium saucepan, bring 2 cups (448 grams) water and the salt to a boil over high heat.

2 In a medium bowl, whisk the polenta into the remaining 2 cups (448 grams) cold water, then whisk into the boiling water and bring to a boil. Reduce the heat to low and simmer, whisking often, being sure to reach the corners of the pot, until the polenta is thick and smooth, about 40 minutes.

3 Remove the polenta from the heat and whisk in the butter. Serve immediately, with peaches and honey.

Milk Toasts: Comfort in a Bowl

WHEN I WAS A LITTLE GIRL, MY MOTHER FED ME HARD ZWIEBACK OR HOLLAND RUSKS SOAKED IN MILK FOR BREAKFAST AND I LOVED IT. LATER IN LIFE, I RECALLED THIS TREAT as I dipped toast into soft-boiled eggs or a creamy sauce. That was how I rediscovered milk toast. Soothing, comforting, delicious milk toast.

Milk toast has been around for years and spans many cultures. It's nothing more than toasted and buttered bread placed in a bowl, covered with warm milk, and sweetened with fruit, maple syrup, sugar, or honey. The result is at once warming and light. It is a great way to use up leftover bread.

The best bread for milk toast is, of course, homemade, but great bakery bread works too. In either case, stale left-over bread beats fresh. Choose a loaf that can stand up to soaking. Breads with fine, tender textures work well; chewy, holey loaves, not so much. Once you have the right bread, cut it into 1-inch-thick slices and toast it. Butter the toasts immediately. Place the warm toasts in bowls that hold a single slice, add warm milk, and flavor with one of my beloved combinations below, or create your own.

Toasted and buttered sliced Challah Loaves (page 145) or bakery-bought brioche, warm whole milk, sliced bananas, sliced strawberries, and sugar.

Toasted and buttered sliced Apple-Cinnamon Bread (page 143) or bakery-bought cinnamon bread, warm whole milk, maple syrup, and Plum Preserves (page 174) or store-bought plum jam (photo above).

Toasted and buttered sliced bakery-bought raisin bread, warm whole milk, sliced fresh apricots, and Apricot Spread (page 177) or store-bought apricot preserves.

Morning Crunch Granola

Makes about 16 cups

This granola formula is my favorite and it makes enough to last for a couple of weeks in most households. There is plenty of room for improvisation, both with the mix-ins (see the variations below) and when serving. I often top the granola with sliced bananas, fresh strawberries, or any seasonal fruit that I have on hand.

Vegetable oil, for the roasting pan
4 cups (464 grams) sliced raw almonds
1 cup (149 grams) raw hulled sunflower seeds
½ cup (170 grams) honey
½ cup (146 grams) pure maple syrup
7 cups (721 grams) old-fashioned rolled oats
1 cup (60 grams) wheat bran
1 cup (100 grams) unsweetened desiccated coconut
1 cup (160 grams) raisins
Milk or plain yogurt, for serving

1 Position a rack in the center of the oven and preheat to 350°F. Lightly oil a large roasting pan.

2 Spread the almonds on a half-sheet pan. Bake, stirring occasionally, until the almonds are lightly toasted, 8 to 12 minutes. Transfer to a large bowl and set aside.

3 Spread the sunflower seeds on the same pan. Bake, stirring occasionally, until lightly toasted, 8 to 12 minutes. Transfer to the bowl of almonds.

4 In a small bowl, stir the honey and maple syrup to combine. Place the oats in the prepared roasting pan, drizzle with the honey mixture, and toss with your hands to coat thoroughly. Bake, stirring occasionally, until the oats are lightly toasted, 15 to 20 minutes. Add the oats to the bowl of almonds and sunflower seeds and cool completely.

5 Stir the bran, coconut, and raisins into the almond mixture. The granola can be stored in an airtight container at room temperature for up to 1 month. Serve the granola with milk or yogurt.

Pecan-Sour Cherry Granola: Substitute chopped pecans for the almonds and chopped dried sour cherries for the raisins.

Pumpkin Seed and Dried Strawberry Granola: Add raw pepitas (hulled pumpkin seeds) and substitute freeze-dried strawberries for the raisins (photo opposite).

Granola Bars

Makes 16 bars

To keep these bars on the healthy side, I avoided adding butter or oil to the oat mixture. But then my baker instincts kicked in. I love streusel and could put it on anything. So I did. A layer of streusel on top crowns the nutty base and jammy middle. It turns out that it's just the thing for "healthy" granola bars. These eat like a dessert, though, crumbling a bit with every bite, so serve them on plates.

BAKER'S NOTE: The baked granola must stand for at least 8 hours before being cut into bars.

Streusel

½ cup (75 grams) stone-ground whole wheat flour
2 tablespoons packed light brown sugar
Pinch of fine sea salt
3 tablespoons unsalted butter, melted and cooled
¼ teaspoon pure vanilla extract

Softened unsalted butter, for the pan
3 cups (309 grams) old-fashioned rolled oats
1 cup (116 grams) sliced almonds, toasted (page 41)
½ cup (75 grams) roasted unsalted peanuts, chopped
¾ cup (109 grams) dried sour cherries, chopped
½ cup (100 grams) dried apricots, chopped
1 cup (340 grams) honey
¼ teaspoon fine sea salt
½ cup (154 grams) Mandarin Orange Spread (page 176), Apricot Spread (page 177), or store-bought Sarabeth's Orange Apricot Marmalade

1 To make the streusel: In a small bowl, mix the flour, brown sugar, salt, butter, and vanilla with your fingers until combined and crumbly. Set aside.

2 Position a rack in the center of the oven and preheat to 350°F. Butter a 13 by 9 by 1¼-inch baking pan. Line with parchment paper, leaving an overhang on all four sides. Butter the parchment.

3 In a large bowl, using your hands, mix the oats, almonds, peanuts, cherries, and apricots with the honey and salt until evenly coated. Transfer to the prepared pan and spread in an even layer. Butter a nonstick baking mat or sheet of parchment paper and place on top of the mixture. Press down very firmly to pack the mixture into an even layer. Uncover and spread the mixture evenly with the orange spread. Sprinkle the streusel on top.

4 Bake until golden brown and firm, about 30 minutes. Transfer the pan to a wire rack and let stand for at least 8 hours.

5 Use the parchment paper overhang to carefully lift the baked granola out of the pan and onto a cutting board. Cut lengthwise into 4 even strips and then cut each strip crosswise into 4 bars, for a total of 16 bars. The granola bars can be stored in an airtight container at room temperature for up to 3 days.

Toasting Nuts and Seeds

NUTS AND SEEDS TAKE ON A CRACKLY CRISPNESS WHEN TOASTED. THE OVEN WORKS BEST FOR EVENLY BROWNING NUTS OR SEEDS WITHOUT BURNING THEM. TO TOAST, SPREAD the nuts (see below for hazelnuts) or seeds on a half-sheet pan and bake in a preheated 350°F oven, stirring occasionally, until fragrant and lightly toasted, 8 to 12 minutes. Toast only one variety at a time; different types toast at different rates. Be careful not to burn the nuts or seeds, especially smaller pieces.

To toast hazelnuts, proceed as above, but toast until the skins are cracked and peeling, about 10 minutes. Wrap the nuts in a clean kitchen towel and let stand for 10 minutes. Rub the hazelnuts in the towel to remove the skins. Don't worry if you don't get every last bit of skin off the nuts.

In all cases, cool the nuts completely before chopping. Use a large heavy knife to chop them; it's not a good idea to use a food processor, as the rough handling can make the nuts release their oils. For coarsely chopped nuts, you can simply place the flat side of the knife over the nuts and press down, crushing the nuts under the knife.

Morning Cookies

Makes about 3 dozen cookies

A few years ago, I decided to create a breakfast cookie. It had to be packed with fiber-rich whole grains and seeds and still taste great. I began with our bakery's basic chocolate chip cookie recipe, took out the chocolate, and came up with the quintessential morning treat. It's perfect with your coffee and easy to grab as you're dashing out the door. I have a thing for crispy cookies and I think you are going to love the snappy texture and rich coconut flavor of these. They have become the cookie I choose when cravings strike—and a bestseller at my bakeries. If you're not in the mood to bake a batch, stop by and buy a bunch.

BAKER'S NOTE: If you don't have four half-sheet pans, let your pans cool completely before baking the next batches.

1 cup (142 grams) unbleached all-purpose flour
¾ teaspoon baking soda
½ teaspoon fine sea salt
1 cup (103 grams) old-fashioned rolled oats
1 cup (64 grams) finely crushed shredded wheat cereal, preferably Barbara's
½ cup (75 grams) stone-ground whole wheat flour
½ cup (50 grams) unsweetened desiccated coconut
⅛ teaspoon freshly grated nutmeg
1 teaspoon pure vanilla extract
1 teaspoon freshly grated lemon zest
⅔ cup (131 grams) superfine sugar
⅔ cup (131 grams) packed light brown sugar
8 tablespoons (114 grams) unsalted butter, cut into ½-inch cubes, at room temperature
2 large eggs, beaten, at room temperature

1 Position the racks in the center and top third of the oven and preheat to 350°F. Line four half-sheet pans with parchment paper.

2 In a medium bowl, whisk the all-purpose flour, baking soda, and salt. Add the oats, shredded wheat cereal, whole wheat flour, coconut, and nutmeg and mix well with your fingertips. In another medium bowl, rub the vanilla and lemon zest into the superfine and brown sugars until well combined.

3 In the bowl of a heavy-duty stand mixer fitted with the paddle attachment, beat the butter on medium-high speed until smooth, about 1 minute. Gradually add the sugar mixture and continue beating, scraping the sides of the bowl often with a silicone spatula, until the mixture is smooth, about 2 minutes. Gradually beat in the eggs, scraping the sides of the bowl occasionally. Reduce the mixer speed to low and gradually add the flour mixture, beating until just combined.

4 Using a 1½-inch-diameter ice-cream scoop, portion the cookie dough onto the prepared pans, placing the cookies about 1½ inches apart. Cover the cookies on one pan with a clean sheet of parchment paper, put another half-sheet pan on top, and press to flatten the cookies to a ⅓-inch thickness. Remove the top pan and parchment and repeat with the remaining pans.

5 Bake the cookies two pans at a time, switching and rotating the positions of the pans halfway through, until light golden brown, 15 to 17 minutes. Cool completely on the pans on wire racks. The cookies can be stored in an airtight container at room temperature for up to 1 week.

Knekkebrød

Seeded Whole-Grain Crackers

Makes 3 half-sheet pans

I'm a cracker person. Not flaky salted baking soda crackers, but grainy, crunchy, wheaty things. My brother Mel knows this about me. That's why he was excited to tell me about the crackers he ate for breakfast while attending a conference in Norway. Every morning, he'd enjoy hearty crackers packed with seeds. When he asked the restaurant for the recipe, he realized what they gave him was already all over the internet. He showed me what he'd found and told me the essential ingredients, and I set about creating my own formula and technique. I'm not sure if they're just like the ones Mel tasted, but I love them.

1⅓ cups (200 grams) stone-ground whole wheat flour
2 cups (206 grams) old-fashioned rolled oats
⅔ cup (99 grams) raw hulled sunflower seeds
⅓ cup (50 grams) sesame seeds
¼ cup (50 grams) flaxseeds
1 teaspoon fine sea salt
1½ cups (336 grams) cold water

1 Position racks in the center and top and bottom thirds of the oven and preheat to 325°F. If you have only two oven racks, bake two pans first and then bake the third.

2 In a large bowl, stir the flour, oats, sunflower seeds, sesame seeds, flaxseeds, and salt together. Add the cold water and stir until a thick, sticky dough forms. Cover loosely with plastic wrap and let stand for 10 minutes.

3 Divide the dough into 3 equal pieces. Place 1 piece on a nonstick baking mat or an 11 by 16-inch sheet of parchment paper. Place an 11 by 16-inch sheet of parchment paper on top of the dough and roll the dough to a 1⁄16-inch thickness. The shape can be organic, with ragged edges. Slide the dough onto a half-sheet pan and peel off the top piece of parchment. Repeat with the remaining dough.

4 Bake the crackers, switching and rotating the positions of the pans halfway through, until dry and light golden brown, about 45 minutes. Cool completely on the pans on wire racks.

5 Break the crackers into pieces. The crackers can be stored in an airtight container at room temperature for up to 1 month.

Cornbread

Makes 1 loaf; 10 to 12 servings

Ages ago, I tasted the cornbread at Angelica Kitchen in New York City's East Village and fell in love with it. It was so tasty I couldn't believe it was vegan. When I created my own grainy cornbread, I also made it without eggs, but I decided to use butter for its incomparable creaminess. This moist whole-grain loaf is not too sweet, so the flavor of the cornmeal shines. For quick breakfasts, I toast slices and simply slather them with butter or almond butter. For a hearty brunch, I top the slices with avocado, tomato, and bacon.

Softened unsalted butter, for the pan

2 cups (320 grams) very finely ground yellow cornmeal

½ cup (75 grams) stone-ground whole wheat flour

½ cup (71 grams) unbleached all-purpose flour

2 tablespoons chickpea flour

1 tablespoon baking powder

½ teaspoon ground ginger

¼ teaspoon freshly grated nutmeg

½ teaspoon fine sea salt

2 cups (448 grams) unsweetened apple juice

8 tablespoons (114 grams) unsalted butter, melted and cooled

½ cup (146 grams) pure maple syrup

1 tablespoon apple cider vinegar

1 Position a rack in the center of the oven and preheat to 350°F. Butter a 9 by 5 by 3-inch loaf pan.

2 In a large bowl, whisk the cornmeal, whole wheat flour, all-purpose flour, chickpea flour, baking powder, ginger, nutmeg, and salt.

3 In a medium bowl, whisk the apple juice, melted butter, maple syrup, and vinegar. Add to the dry ingredients and fold in with the whisk until well mixed. Let stand for 5 minutes, then scrape the batter into the pan. Smooth the top with an offset spatula.

4 Bake until golden brown on top and a cake tester inserted into the center of the cornbread comes out clean, 45 to 50 minutes. Cool in the pan on a wire rack for 15 minutes, then turn out of the pan and cool completely on the rack.

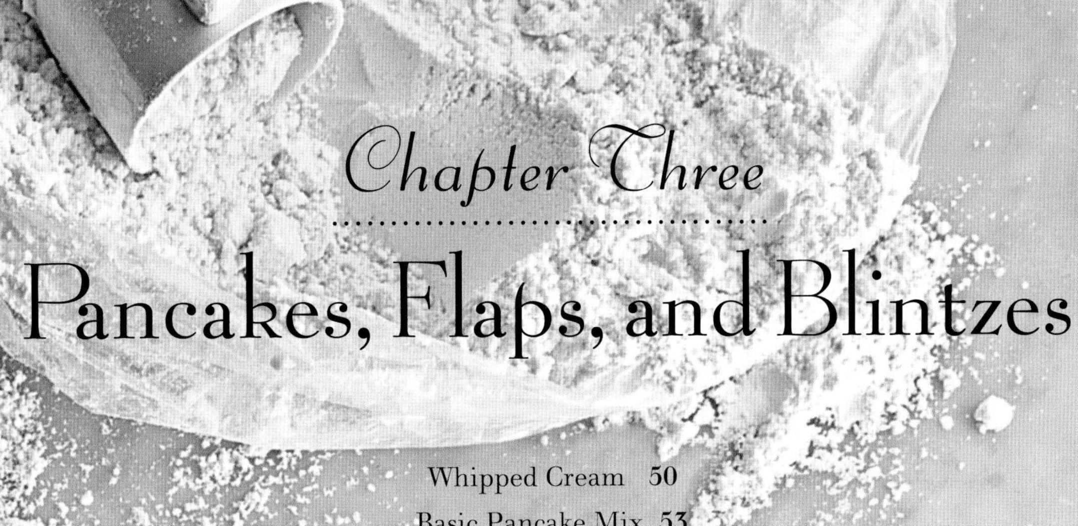

Chapter Three

Pancakes, Flaps, and Blintzes

MY HOTCAKES FALL INTO THREE GROUPS: TALL AND FLUFFY PANCAKES, FLAT AND SPRINGY "FLAPS", AND THIN, DELICATE BLINTZES. Though their thicknesses and textures vary, they share the perfect technique for a quick morning treat: Simply make a batter and cook it on the stovetop for a few minutes. The resulting skillet cakes aren't too sugary, so you can sweeten them to taste with syrup and other toppings.

My favorite way to enjoy all three is with my fingers. I love the wheaty goodness of pancakes so much that I eat them like bread, spread with butter. I roll them up into "cigars" and dip them, bite by bite, into a little dish of maple syrup, getting just enough for a hint of sweetness. I do the same for flaps, but I add a little brown sugar to that layer of butter and skip the syrup. When I make blintzes, the thinnest of the pancake family, I sometimes tear the delicate paper-thin rounds into strips and enjoy them plain. I assume you will eat all of these in a more conventional fashion, but I hope you try them my way just once—food tastes better when you touch it.

KEY INGREDIENTS

Pure Maple Syrup: Avoid "pancake syrup" and other imitation syrups at all cost. The real thing tastes best. Grade A is technically the highest quality, as it's the most refined and clear, but the intensity of Grades B and C is appealing too. You can choose dark amber for more robust maple notes or light amber for a subtler taste.

Whipped Cream: Always make your own—it's far more delicious than anything from a can or tub. It's also incredibly fast and easy.

Whipped Cream

Makes 2 cups

SET A MEDIUM BOWL IN A LARGE BOWL FILLED WITH ICE AND WATER AND ADD 1 CUP (232 GRAMS) WELL-CHILLED HEAVY CREAM. WHIP WITH A HANDHELD ELECTRIC MIXER on high speed until the cream is lightly thickened and the beater leaves a trail on the surface. Gradually add 3 tablespoons superfine sugar and the seeds from ¼ vanilla bean, preferably a Plumped Vanilla Bean (page 3), or ¼ teaspoon pure vanilla extract. Beat just until soft peaks form. Use immediately, or cover and refrigerate for up to 2 hours. Lightly whisk again just before serving.

TOOL KIT

Griddle: You don't need a griddle, but with one you can make big batches quickly. The best is a two-burner cast-iron stovetop model. Cast iron heats the most evenly, but it must be seasoned before use and then regularly with use to create a natural nonstick surface. Electric countertop griddles have a large cooking area, are available with a variety of surface options, and are convenient for serving at the table. If you don't want to get a griddle, use two skillets to turn out large batches quickly.

Crepe Pan: Flaps cook especially well in a well-seasoned crepe pan, which has a flat base and low sides for easy flipping and turning. If you don't have one, use a nonstick skillet.

Pancake Turner: Also known simply as a spatula. Be sure to use one that is as large or almost as large as the pancakes (about 4 inches wide); it should also be offset, sturdy, and thin. If you're using a nonstick pan, be sure to use a silicone spatula that won't scratch the surface.

Silicone Pastry Brush: These brushes can withstand high heat, making them ideal for greasing hot griddles and skillets. You can find them in kitchenware shops.

Ice-Cream Scoop: A 2-inch-diameter ice-cream scoop with a scant ⅓-cup capacity is the perfect size for forming pancakes. It makes the process mess-free and results in perfect rounds.

TIPS FOR PERFECT PANCAKES

1 Don't overmix pancake batter. If you do, you'll end up with tough, rubbery pancakes. To avoid stirring too much, first mix the dry and wet ingredients separately, then combine them and stir just until the batter is barely smooth. A few lumps or wisps of flour should remain; they will disappear as you use the batter. If you are adding other ingredients to the batter, such as blueberries, you can leave the batter quite lumpy, as it will undergo further stirring when you mix in these ingredients.

2 Let the batter stand for a few minutes while you heat the griddle or skillet. This allows the gluten in the batter to relax and gives the flour lumps time to hydrate and begin to dissolve, to yield more tender pancakes. If the batter gets too thick as it stands, fold in a little additional milk to return it to its original consistency.

3 Heat the griddle or skillet thoroughly before pouring on the batter. Here is a surefire test for checking the temperature of the griddle: Dip your fingers in cold water and flick the droplets over the griddle. If the water forms balls that skitter and dance briefly before evaporating, the temperature is right.

4 I use Clarified Butter (page 54) for greasing the griddle or skillet. You could use vegetable oil, but it lacks the flavor and browning ability of clarified butter, which can stand up to high temperatures. To grease, give the surface a light, even coat with a silicone pastry brush; you don't want the food to fry in pools of butter.

5 For perfectly round pancakes, scoop ⅓ cup batter onto the preheated griddle or skillet with a 2-inch-diameter ice-cream scoop or ⅓-cup dry measuring cup and gently spread it with the underside of the scoop or cup into a 4-inch round.

6 It's a good idea to do a test pancake to check the temperature of the cooking surface. Then proceed with the rest of the batch, adjusting the heat as necessary to brown the outsides evenly while cooking the insides through. Flip the pancakes carefully (you don't get extra points for tossing pancakes high in the air). Cook them just until the bottom is golden and bubbles appear on the surface before flipping them, and don't flip them more than once, or they will lose volume.

7 For the most delicious results, serve griddle cakes as soon as they come off the heat. I stay at the stove while my grandkids line up for their pancakes and keep dishing the pancakes out as they are cooked until the batter is used up. If absolutely necessary, you can keep pancakes warm for up to 10 minutes on a parchment paper–lined half-sheet pan in a preheated 200°F oven.

8 Have the toppings waiting on the breakfast table. That way, your family and friends can quickly serve themselves. With the exception of whipped cream, it's important to serve toppings warm or at room temperature. It's not pretty to think about cold butter trying to melt on hot pancakes. Ideally the plates should be warm too. Simply heat them in a preheated 200°F oven for a few minutes.

A NOTE ON SERVING SIZES: I give the number of pancakes that each recipe makes, but it isn't easy to translate that number into the number of servings. It's a question of appetite—kids may want only one or two pancakes, dads may want four.

Basic Pancake Mix

Makes about 6 cups; enough for about 3 dozen pancakes

If you keep a batch of this buttery homemade mix in your refrigerator or freezer, you can whip up fresh from-scratch pancakes (page 57) or flaps (page 67) any weekday morning. There's always a bag of this mix in my freezer. I love how it delivers the flavors of a leisurely made meal in minutes.

4½ cups (639 grams) unbleached all-purpose flour

3 tablespoons baking powder

1¼ teaspoons fine sea salt

12 tablespoons (171 grams) unsalted butter, cut into ½-inch cubes and chilled

1 In the bowl of a heavy-duty stand mixer fitted with the paddle attachment, mix the flour, baking powder, and salt on medium-low speed until well combined, about 1 minute. Add the butter and toss with your fingers until coated with the flour, then mix on medium speed until the consistency of fine meal, about 10 minutes. This takes a long time because the butter should be totally absorbed, with no butter chips showing at all.

2 The mix can be used immediately or refrigerated in an airtight container for up to 2 weeks or frozen for up to 1 month.

Clarified Butter

Makes about 1½ cups

I CAN THINK OF VERY FEW DOWNSIDES TO BUTTER. ITS FLAVOR IS UNMATCHED—MARGARINE IS NOT AN OPTION FOR ME. BUTTER'S ONLY POSSIBLE AREA FOR IMPROVEMENT is its low burning temperature. Butter is mostly fat, with a small amount of milk solids and water; use high-fat butters for a better yield. If you heat butter in a skillet or griddle, eventually the milk solids will burn and the fat will smoke. Food cooked in burned butter will taste burned. If the milk solids are removed from the butter, though, the remaining fat can be heated to much higher temperatures without burning.

Clarified butter is just that—butter with the milk solids removed. The process is very easy: Boil the butter to evaporate some of the water and separate the milk solids from the fat. The resulting clarified butter can then be chilled until firm. At our restaurants, where we clarify pounds of butter a day, we prefer the double-boiler method, which eliminates any chance of burning. At home, where you can stand by the stove for the few minutes required, you may prefer to use the quick-method variation, over direct heat, given below. Clarified butter is a must for greasing a griddle or waffle iron and it can be used like any cooking fat for sautéing or panfrying.

1 pound (454 grams) unsalted butter, cut into ½-inch cubes

1 Put the butter in the top of a double boiler. Place over simmering water in the bottom of the double boiler and melt the butter, stirring occasionally and skimming off any foam from the surface. This could take about 20 minutes.

2 Pour all of the melted butter into a pint container and cool, uncovered, to room temperature. Then cover tightly and chill until the butter is firm, at least 2 hours, or up to overnight.

3 Using the handle of a wooden spoon, poke a hole through the firm butter, reaching down to the bottom of the container. Pour off the milky liquid, leaving the yellow clarified butter in the container. The clarified butter can be refrigerated in the same airtight container, covered, for up to 3 weeks.

Quick Clarified Butter: In a medium saucepan, bring the butter to a full boil over medium heat and cook for 30 seconds. Remove from the heat and let stand for 5 minutes. Skim the foam off the top of the butter and discard. Then pour the clarified butter into a small bowl, leaving the solids behind in the pan. Use immediately, or let cool for 20 minutes, then cover and refrigerate for up to 3 weeks.

Classic Buttermilk Pancakes

Makes about 12 pancakes; 4 to 6 servings

They're classic for a reason: As tasty as added flavors may be, the comforting familiarity of buttermilk pancakes makes them the ones we all crave. The buttermilk brings a hint of tanginess and a tender texture to my all-purpose pancake batter. I still use whole milk in the mixture for its distinctive subtle creaminess. Together, those milks blend into the perfect version of traditional pancakes.

2 large eggs

1 cup (224 grams) whole milk

½ cup (112 grams) low-fat buttermilk

2 tablespoons superfine sugar

1 teaspoon pure vanilla extract

2 cups (284 grams) Basic Pancake Mix (page 53)

1 tablespoon Clarified Butter (page 54) or vegetable oil, as needed

Softened unsalted butter, for serving

Warm pure maple syrup or fruit syrup (page 167), for serving

1 In a medium bowl, whisk the eggs until broken. Whisk in the milk, buttermilk, sugar, and vanilla until blended.

2 Place the pancake mix in a large bowl. Make a well in the center and pour in the egg mixture. Gently fold in with a whisk until just combined. Don't overbeat, or the pancakes will end up tough and gummy.

3 Heat a well-seasoned cast-iron or nonstick griddle or skillet over medium-low heat. Brush with clarified butter to lightly coat, then wipe off any excess with a clean kitchen or paper towel. Using a 2-inch-diameter ice-cream scoop or dry measuring cup (scant ⅓ cup) for each pancake, portion the batter onto the griddle, leaving an inch or so between the pancakes. Gently spread each into a 4-inch round with the back of the scoop or cup and cook until tiny bubbles appear on the surface, about 2 minutes. Carefully turn the pancakes and cook until the other side is golden brown, about 2 more minutes. Serve immediately, or keep warm on a half-sheet pan lined with parchment paper in a preheated 200°F oven. Repeat with the remaining batter.

4 Serve hot, with softened butter and warm syrup.

Blueberry Pancakes: Fold 2 cups (284 grams) fresh blueberries into the batter, being careful not to overmix. Serve hot, with warm maple syrup, and top with a few fresh blueberries (photo opposite).

Sarabeth's Whole Wheat Pancakes

Makes about 16 pancakes; 6 to 8 servings

To my taste, these are the ultimate pancakes. I make a batch whenever my grandkids come to visit. They've voted it the hands-down winner—and they don't even realize there's whole wheat flour in the batter. Because the pancakes are not too sweet, they leave room for as much syrup as you like. This versatile recipe also allows for plenty of variations, from apricot-almond to wheat berry pancakes to your own creations.

2 tablespoons superfine sugar

½ teaspoon packed freshly grated orange zest

1 cup (150 grams) whole wheat flour

1 cup (142 grams) unbleached all-purpose flour

1 tablespoon baking powder

½ teaspoon fine sea salt

2 large eggs, separated

1½ cups (336 grams) whole milk

1 tablespoon unsalted butter, melted and cooled

1 teaspoon pure vanilla extract

1 tablespoon Clarified Butter (page 54) or vegetable oil, or as needed

Softened unsalted butter, for serving

Warm pure maple syrup or fruit syrup (page 167), for serving

1 In a large bowl, combine the sugar and orange zest and rub together with your fingertips. Whisk in the whole wheat flour, all-purpose flour, baking powder, and salt.

2 In a medium bowl, whisk the egg yolks, milk, butter, and vanilla until smooth. Make a well in the center of the dry ingredients and pour in the milk mixture. Gently fold with the whisk until just combined. Don't overbeat, or the pancakes will end up tough and gummy.

3 In a clean large bowl, using a clean whisk, beat the egg whites until soft peaks form. Fold one-third of the whites into the batter to loosen it. With a silicone spatula, gently fold in the remaining whites in two batches until just incorporated.

4 Heat a well-seasoned cast-iron or nonstick griddle or skillet over medium-low heat. Brush with clarified butter to lightly coat, and wipe off any excess with a clean kitchen or paper towel. Using a 2-inch-diameter ice-cream scoop or dry measuring cup (scant ⅓ cup) for each pancake, portion the batter onto the griddle, leaving an inch or so between the pancakes. Gently spread each into a 4-inch round with the back of the scoop or cup and cook until tiny bubbles appear on the surface, about 2 minutes. Carefully turn the pancakes and cook until

the other side is golden brown, about 2 more minutes. Serve immediately, or keep warm on a half-sheet pan lined with parchment paper in a preheated 200°F oven. Repeat with the remaining batter.

5 Serve hot, with softened butter and warm syrup.

Apricot-Almond Pancakes: Fold ½ cup (58 grams) sliced almonds, toasted (page 41) and coarsely chopped, into the batter. Serve the pancakes topped with sliced fresh apricots or a spoonful of Apricot Spread (page 177).

Wheat Berry Pancakes: Fold ½ cup (50 grams) drained Cooked Wheat Berries (page 32) into the batter. Serve the pancakes topped with softened butter and warm syrup.

Oatmeal Pancakes

Makes about 12 pancakes; 4 to 6 servings

Bananas and oatmeal are a great combination, as anyone who has sliced bananas on top of oatmeal can attest. In this recipe, the oats contribute texture and grainy flavor and the bananas add sweetness. The pancakes are very quick to make and just the thing for a healthful family meal. Remove the yogurt from the refrigerator about 30 minutes before serving so it loses its chill.

1¼ cups (129 grams) old-fashioned rolled oats

1¼ cups (178 grams) unbleached all-purpose flour

2 tablespoons superfine sugar

2 teaspoons baking powder

⅛ teaspoon packed freshly grated nutmeg

¼ teaspoon fine sea salt

2 large eggs

1½ cups (336 grams) whole milk

2 teaspoons unsalted butter, melted

1 teaspoon pure vanilla extract

1 tablespoon Clarified Butter (page 54) or vegetable oil, or as needed

Plain Greek yogurt, at cool room temperature, for serving

Warm pure maple syrup, for serving

Sliced bananas, for serving

1 In a food processor, pulse the oats until finely ground. Transfer to a large bowl and add the flour, sugar, baking powder, nutmeg, and salt. Whisk until well blended.

2 In a medium bowl, whisk the eggs until broken. Whisk in the milk, butter, and vanilla until just blended. Make a well in the center of the dry ingredients and pour in the egg mixture. Gently fold with a whisk until just combined. Don't overbeat, or the pancakes will end up tough and gummy. Let the batter sit for 10 minutes.

3 Heat a well-seasoned cast-iron or nonstick griddle or skillet over medium-low heat. Brush with clarified butter to lightly coat, and wipe off any excess with a clean kitchen or paper towel. Using a 2-inch-diameter ice-cream scoop or dry measuring cup (scant ⅓ cup) for each pancake, portion the batter onto the griddle, leaving an inch or so between the pancakes. Gently spread each into a 4-inch round with the back of the scoop or cup and cook until tiny bubbles appear on the surface, about 2 minutes. Carefully turn the pancakes and cook until the other side is golden brown, about 2 more minutes. Serve immediately, or keep warm on a half-sheet pan lined with parchment paper in a preheated 200°F oven. Repeat with the remaining batter.

4 Serve hot, with yogurt, warm syrup, and bananas.

Corn Pancakes

Makes about 14 pancakes; 4 to 6 servings

For those who can't resist the sweet flavor of corn in the morning, I offer corn pancakes. My secret is combining corn kernels with fine cornmeal. Organic cornmeal has the best taste because it is usually stone-ground from flavorful corn; the metal rollers used to grind mass-produced cornmeal heat the meal, diminishing its flavor. Warmed honey is the perfect topping for these sunny yellow hotcakes.

¾ cup (107 grams) unbleached all-purpose flour

¾ cup (120 grams) very finely ground yellow cornmeal or polenta

2 tablespoons superfine sugar

1 tablespoon baking powder

⅛ teaspoon fine sea salt

2 large eggs

1 cup (224 grams) whole milk

1 tablespoon extra-virgin olive oil

½ cup (2¾ ounces; 79 grams) fresh or drained canned corn kernels

1 tablespoon Clarified Butter (page 54) or vegetable oil, or as needed

Softened unsalted butter, for serving

Warm honey, for serving

1 In a large bowl, whisk the flour, cornmeal, sugar, baking powder, and salt. In a medium bowl, whisk the eggs until broken. Whisk in the milk and olive oil until just blended. Make a well in the center of the dry ingredients and pour in the egg mixture. Gently fold with a whisk until just combined. Don't overbeat, or the pancakes will end up tough and gummy. Using a silicone spatula, gently fold in the corn until evenly distributed.

2 Heat a well-seasoned cast-iron or nonstick griddle or skillet over medium-low heat. Brush with clarified butter to lightly coat, and wipe off any excess with a clean kitchen or paper towel. Using a 2-inch-diameter ice-cream scoop or dry measuring cup (scant ⅓ cup) for each pancake, portion the batter onto the griddle, leaving an inch or so between the pancakes. Gently spread each into a 4-inch round with the back of the scoop or cup and cook until tiny bubbles appear on the surface, about 2 minutes. Carefully turn the pancakes and cook until the other side is golden brown, about 2 more minutes. Serve immediately, or keep warm on a half-sheet pan lined with parchment paper in a preheated 200°F oven. Repeat with the remaining batter.

3 Serve hot, with softened butter and warm honey.

Blueberry-Corn Pancakes: Fold 1 cup (142 grams) blueberries into the batter when you add the corn.

White Cheddar Pancakes
with Sautéed Apples

Makes about 20 pancakes; 6 to 8 servings

The Yankee tradition of pairing Cheddar cheese and apples is put to excellent use in these flapjacks. An extra-sharp white Cheddar, such as one from Vermont's Cabot Cheese collective, is needed to stand up to the flavorful apples and maple syrup. The sautéed apples, which are sensational with these pancakes, pair well with waffles and French toast too.

COOK'S NOTE: If you can't find Jonagold apples, use another variety that is sweet-tart, firm, and crunchy.

Apples

2 tablespoons Clarified Butter (page 54)

6 large Jonagold apples (2½ pounds; 1.2 kilograms), peeled, cored, and cut into ¼-inch-thick wedges

¼ cup (49 grams) packed light brown sugar

1½ tablespoons fresh lemon juice

¼ teaspoon ground cinnamon

⅛ teaspoon ground cardamom, preferably freshly ground

Seeds from ½ vanilla bean, preferably a Plumped Vanilla Bean (page 3), or ½ teaspoon pure vanilla extract

2 cups (284 grams) unbleached all-purpose flour

1 tablespoon superfine sugar

2 teaspoons baking powder

½ teaspoon fine sea salt

1¾ cups (392 grams) whole milk

2 large eggs, separated

1½ cups (142 grams) packed shredded extra-sharp Cheddar cheese, preferably Vermont

1 tablespoon Clarified Butter (page 54) or vegetable oil, or as needed

1 To prepare the apples: In a very large skillet, heat the clarified butter over medium heat. Add the apple slices and cook, stirring occasionally, until barely tender, 8 to 10 minutes.

2 Gently stir in the brown sugar, lemon juice, cinnamon, and cardamom and cook until the apples are tender and syrupy, 2 to 3 minutes. Stir in the vanilla seeds. Keep warm over very low heat.

3 To make the pancakes: In a large bowl, whisk the flour, superfine sugar, baking powder, and salt. In a medium bowl, whisk the milk and egg yolks until smooth. Make a well in the center of the dry ingredients and pour in the milk mixture. Gently fold with the whisk until just combined. Don't overbeat, or the pancakes will end up tough and gummy.

4 In a clean large bowl, using a clean whisk, beat the egg whites until soft peaks form. Fold one-third of the whites into the batter to loosen it. With a silicone spatula, gently fold in the remaining whites in two batches until almost incorporated, with some white streaks remaining. Gently fold in the cheese until evenly distributed.

5 Heat a well-seasoned cast-iron or nonstick griddle or skillet over medium-low heat. Brush with clarified butter to lightly coat, and wipe off any excess with a clean kitchen or paper towel. Using a 2-inch-diameter ice-cream scoop or dry measuring cup (scant ⅓ cup) for each pancake, portion the batter onto the griddle, leaving an inch or so between the pancakes. Gently spread each into a 4-inch round with the back of the scoop or cup and cook until tiny bubbles appear on the surface of the batter, about 2 minutes. Carefully turn the pancakes and cook until the other side is golden brown, about 2 more minutes. Serve immediately, or keep warm on a half-sheet pan lined with parchment paper in a preheated 200°F oven. Repeat with the remaining batter.

6 Serve hot, with the warm apples.

Souffléd Lemon-Ricotta Pancakes

Makes about 18 pancakes; 6 to 8 servings

These creamy, lemony pancakes rise into light-as-air puffs. You get the ethereal delicacy of a soufflé in minutes with these quick skillet pancakes. The tissue-thin golden "skin" encases a luxurious silken center. These pancakes are a more delicate version of what we serve in our restaurants. (Given the huge numbers of orders we get during the brunch rush, we can't separate and beat the eggs for each batch as directed here.) Be sure to use high-quality fresh ricotta, as its rich flavor is the foundation of the batter.

1¼ cups (178 grams) unbleached all-purpose flour
2 teaspoons baking powder
⅛ teaspoon packed freshly grated nutmeg
⅛ teaspoon fine sea salt
5 large eggs, separated
1⅓ cups (340 grams) fresh whole-milk ricotta
4 teaspoons superfine sugar
1 teaspoon packed freshly grated lemon zest
1 teaspoon pure vanilla extract
⅔ cup (149 grams) whole milk
2 tablespoons unsalted butter, melted
1 tablespoon Clarified Butter (page 54) or vegetable oil, or as needed
Confectioners' sugar, for dusting
Meyer Lemon Maple Syrup (page 169), for serving
Raspberries, for serving

1 Sift the flour, baking powder, nutmeg, and salt into a medium bowl. In a large bowl, whisk the egg yolks, ricotta, sugar, lemon zest, and vanilla until smooth, then whisk in the milk and butter until well combined. Add half of the dry ingredients and gently fold in with the whisk until just incorporated. Fold in the remaining dry ingredients.

2 In a clean large bowl, using a clean whisk, beat the egg whites until medium peaks form. Fold one-third of the whites into the batter to loosen it. With a silicone spatula, gently fold in the remaining whites in two batches until just incorporated.

3 Heat a well-seasoned cast-iron or nonstick griddle or skillet over medium-low heat. Brush with clarified butter to lightly coat, and wipe off any excess with a clean kitchen or paper towel. Using a 2-inch-diameter ice-cream scoop or dry measuring cup (scant ⅓ cup) for each pancake, scoop the batter onto the griddle, leaving an inch or so between the pancakes. Don't touch the pancakes! They are very delicate and can collapse if disturbed. Cook until the bottom is light golden brown, 2 to 3 minutes. Carefully turn the pancakes and cook until the other side is golden brown, 2 to 3 more minutes. Serve immediately, or keep warm on a half-sheet pan lined with parchment paper in a preheated 200°F oven. Repeat with the remaining batter.

4 Dust with confectioners' sugar and serve hot, with syrup and raspberries.

Basic Flaps

Makes about 12 flaps; 4 to 6 servings

You may be wondering what a flap is. I wanted a flapjack that was as cakey as a pancake but not as thick. I didn't want it as thin or as eggy as crepes or blintzes though, and I certainly didn't want a bready texture. After testing a number of batters, I hit the jackpot. Using my basic mix, I created a pancake that managed to stay fluffy despite its flatness. It looked beautiful and was easy to roll up. When I realized it was perfect for filling and rolling up like a wrap, I decided to name it a flap.

As much as I love stuffing flaps, I also really enjoy them with a simple spread of butter and brown sugar. The combination reminds me of the breakfasts I enjoyed in the crepe houses in Ghent, Belgium. That topping also reminds me that sometimes, simpler is better. Butter and brown sugar are all you need to enjoy delicious flaps.

2 large eggs

1¼ cups (280 grams) whole milk

½ cup (112 grams) low-fat buttermilk

2 tablespoons superfine sugar

1 teaspoon pure vanilla extract

2 cups (284 grams) Basic Pancake Mix (page 53)

1 tablespoon Clarified Butter (page 54) or vegetable oil, or as needed

Softened unsalted butter, for serving

Brown sugar, for serving

1 In a medium bowl, whisk the eggs until broken. Whisk in the milk, buttermilk, superfine sugar, and vanilla until just blended.

2 Place the pancake mix in a large bowl. Make a well in the center and pour in the egg mixture. Stir with a whisk until smooth.

3 Heat a well-seasoned 9-inch crepe pan or nonstick skillet over medium heat. Brush with clarified butter to lightly coat, and wipe off any excess with a clean kitchen or paper towel. Using a 2-inch-diameter ice-cream scoop or dry measuring cup, pour a generous ⅓ cup batter into the pan, tilting the pan from side to side and in a circular motion until the batter coats the bottom. Cook only until the underside of the flap begins to brown lightly, 1 to 2 minutes. Using a spatula, carefully lift the flap and quickly turn it over. Cook until the underside is lightly brown, 1 to 2 minutes. Serve immediately, or keep warm on a half-sheet pan lined with parchment paper in a preheated 200°F oven. You can fit 2 flaps in a single layer on the pan. Place a sheet of parchment paper between each layer. Repeat with the remaining batter.

4 Serve hot, spread with softened butter and sprinkled with brown sugar.

Flaps with Fried Eggs and Ham: Place 1 thin slice of ham and 1 fried egg on each flap and fold over, leaving some of the egg yolk exposed. Sprinkle with coarsely ground black pepper and serve with grainy mustard (photo page 66).

Flaps with Scallion Scrambled Eggs: Fill each flap with Green-and-White Scrambled Eggs (page 195). Fold over both sides of each flap and roll up from the bottom.

Flap Pinwheels with Scottish Salmon and Cream Cheese: Spread some Goat Cheese Spread (page 171) or softened cream cheese on each flap and top with slices of Scottish smoked salmon. Roll up and trim the ends. Cut into 1-inch-thick slices.

Cheese Blintzes

Makes about 30 blintzes; 8 to 10 servings

Delicate and plump, these cheese blintzes are the best I have ever eaten. The combination of farmer cheese and cream cheese with fresh lemon zest is exceptional. I learned to make these from my mother-in-law, Margaret, who taught me to turn over the blintz skins with my fingers instead of a spatula. Her technique means that you can cook even the thinnest possible skins without tearing them. It also means getting red and tender fingertips, but it's worth it. Once you taste these, you will absolutely agree. Through practice, you will develop the skill for flipping the blintzes quickly and almost painlessly. And you'll find as much pleasure in the cooking process as you will in eating the blintzes.

Filling

1½ pounds (680 grams) farmer cheese, softened
1 pound (454 grams) cream cheese, softened
1 teaspoon packed freshly grated lemon zest
⅓ cup (65 grams) superfine sugar
3 large egg yolks

Skins

1 cup (142 grams) unbleached all-purpose flour
¼ teaspoon fine sea salt
1 tablespoon superfine sugar
12 large eggs
3 cups (672 grams) whole milk
3 tablespoons Clarified Butter (page 54)

Confectioners' sugar, for garnish
Chunky Apple Butter (page 181), for serving
Sour cream, for serving

1 To make the filling: In a large bowl, mix the farmer cheese and cream cheese with a silicone spatula until well blended. Stir in the lemon zest and sugar. Gently fold in the egg yolks one at a time, mixing until combined. Cover tightly with plastic wrap and refrigerate for at least 1 hour, or up to 1 day, before using.

2 To make the skins: Line three half-sheet pans with parchment paper. Sift the flour, salt, and sugar into a large bowl. In another large bowl, beat the eggs and milk with a handheld electric mixer until blended. While beating, add the flour mixture in three additions, mixing until smooth.

3 Strain the batter through a fine-mesh sieve into a bowl, pressing any remaining flour lumps through the sieve with a silicone spatula. Scrape any batter from the bottom of the strainer into the bowl. Give it a quick mix to make sure the flour is evenly distributed.

4 Heat an 8½-inch nonstick skillet over medium heat. Brush the skillet very lightly with clarified butter. Ladle ½ cup batter into the pan, tilting the pan from side to side and in a circular motion until the batter coats the bottom and lower sides. Pour the excess batter back into the bowl. (This will form a little scallop on the side of the skin that will serve as a marker for where to place the filling.) Return the skillet to the heat and cook only until the edges of the skin begin to come away from the sides of the pan. Using the thumbs and fingers of both hands, carefully lift the skin and quickly turn it over. (You might want to keep a bowl of cold water and a towel near the stove to cool your fingers down and dry them.) Cook until the underside is just set, 5 to 10 seconds. Transfer to one of the prepared half-sheet pans.

5 Continue making skins until all the batter is used, occasionally stirring the batter and lightly brushing the pan with more clarified butter. You can fit 2 blintzes in a single layer on one half-sheet pan. Place a sheet of parchment paper between each layer, and don't stack more than 5 layers on one pan.

6 To fill the blintz skins: Place a skin on a flat surface with the scalloped edge closest to you and the more attractive smooth side down. Place 2 tablespoons of the filling ½ inch from the scalloped edge and fold that edge over the cheese. Press gently. Fold in both sides of the skin and roll up from the bottom. Place the blintz, seam side down, on a parchment paper–lined half-sheet pan. Continue making blintzes until all the skins and the filling are used up. Cover the filled blintzes tightly with plastic wrap and refrigerate for up to 3 days or freeze for up to 1 month. If frozen, defrost overnight in the refrigerator.

7 To sauté the blintzes: In a large skillet, heat 2 tablespoons clarified butter over medium-low heat. Add only enough blintzes, seam side down, to the pan to fill it without overcrowding. Sauté until the bottoms are golden, about 2 minutes. Turn the blintzes over and cook until the other sides are golden, about 2 more minutes. Serve immediately, or keep warm on a half-sheet pan lined with parchment paper in a preheated 200°F oven. Repeat with the remaining blintzes.

8 To serve: Place 3 blintzes on each plate and dust lightly with confectioners' sugar. Serve hot, with apple butter and sour cream.

Baked Layered Blintzes
with Strawberry-Rhubarb Preserves

Makes 12 servings

Classic stuffed blintzes taste great, but they need to be sautéed to order and served warm. This casserole is a nice, easy way to prepare blintzes for a crowd. You layer the skins with the cheese filling and preserves the way you would a lasagna. Then you simply bake it and serve the blintzes hot from the oven.

2 tablespoons unsalted butter, softened

Cheese Blintzes (page 69), skins unfilled, filling softened

½ cup (154 grams) Strawberry-Rhubarb Preserves (page 175) or store-bought Sarabeth's Strawberry Rhubarb Preserves

1 tablespoon Demerara sugar

1 Preheat the oven to 325°F. Use 1 tablespoon butter to generously grease a 13 by 9 by 2-inch glass or ceramic baking dish.

2 Place 1 blintz skin in each of the four corners of the dish to meet the rim of the dish, cover the sides, and partly cover the bottom. Cut 2 blintz skins in half and arrange the cut sides along the two long sides to completely cover the sides of the dish. Place 2 skins in the bottom of the dish to completely cover it.

3 Using a 1½-inch-diameter ice-cream scoop, drop 12 mounds of cheese filling (using about one-third of the filling) evenly over the blintz skins in the bottom of the dish. With a small offset spatula, very gently spread the filling evenly over the bottom. Dollop ¼ cup preserves over the cheese and very gently spread evenly. Cover the jam with 8 blintz skins, slightly overlapping them to cover the preserves and come up the sides of the dish. Top with half of the remaining cheese filling and the remaining preserves. Cover with another 8 blintz skins and then the remaining cheese filling. Arrange the remaining 6 blintz skins on top to completely cover the filling. Tuck and fold in any overhanging edges as you would a piecrust.

4 Melt the remaining 1 tablespoon butter and gently brush on top of the blintzes. Sprinkle with the sugar. Cover tightly with foil and bake for 20 minutes.

5 Uncover the blintzes and bake until golden brown on top, about 15 minutes longer. Cool to room temperature, then cut into 12 servings.

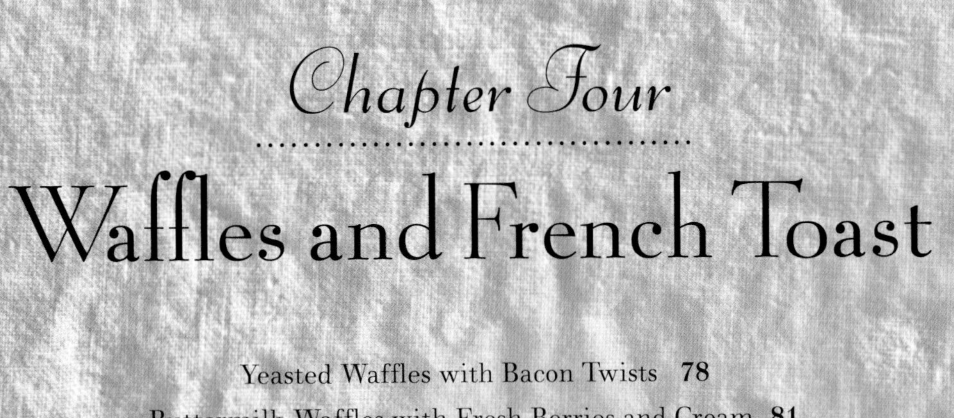

Chapter Four

Waffles and French Toast

WAFFLES AND FRENCH TOAST MAY BE EVEN MORE FUN TO MAKE AND EAT THAN THEIR PANCAKE COUSINS. THE DRAMATIC RISE OF THE batter in the waffle iron seems magical—it never fails to fascinate the youngsters in the house or to bring back memories of childhood breakfasts for the adults. The craters in waffles make for nestling extravagant amounts of melted butter, warm syrup, fruit spreads, or whipped cream. French toast undergoes a similarly spectacular transformation. The bread develops a nearly caramelized outside crust and a rich inside as silky and ethereal as custard.

My recipes for both of these employ unique techniques that I've perfected over the years. Many of my waffle batters start with cutting cold butter into the dry ingredients until the mixture resembles fine crumbs. This technique ensures a light and tender waffle. (A food processor makes short work of this step, but you can also rub the butter into the dry ingredients with a pastry blender or your fingertips.) For my French toast, I thoroughly soak the bread before cooking it both on the stovetop and in the oven. That second step ensures that the custard center cooks through and puffs.

While they are usually considered breakfast food, waffles are terrific for dinner too, and French toast can be special enough for dessert. The yeast, buttermilk, corn, and potato waffles in this chapter are all ideal beginnings for savory dishes. French toast is related to bread pudding but looks even more elegant. A scoop of whipped cream—or, better yet, ice cream—makes it a welcome end to any meal. As versatile as these dishes are, though, I still enjoy them most in the morning. When they're sizzling in clarified butter, their smell alone ensures a great day ahead.

KEY INGREDIENTS

Bread: The better the bread, the better the French toast. A homemade loaf is ideal, so I've provided the recipes: Great Bread (page 138), Challah Loaves (page 145), Apple-Cinnamon Bread (page 143), and Sarabeth's House Bread (page 140). But if you don't have time to bake your own bread, buy handcrafted loaves from a good local bakery. Choose a firm loaf with personality—one you would gladly eat without butter or jam, such as challah, brioche, raisin or apple bread, or a country white or sourdough loaf.

TOOL KIT

Waffle Iron: Stovetop waffle irons may seem tempting, but they are really for Belgian waffles. For good old-fashioned American waffles, use an electric waffle iron with nonstick grids. If you have an old iron with uncoated metal grids, never wash it with soap and water—this will destroy the residual buildup of fat that keeps your next batch from sticking. Just wipe the grids clean with moist paper towels.

Griddle: For French toast, a griddle allows you to make large batches. See page 51 for more information.

TIPS FOR PERFECT WAFFLES

1 Always preheat the waffle iron according to the manufacturer's directions. Each model has a different way of telling you when the iron is hot enough for the batter—sometimes the indicator turns on, sometimes it turns off. Unlike a griddle for pancakes, you won't be able to check the temperature by splashing the grids with water, so just be patient. Allow 10 to 15 minutes for preheating. I always turn on the waffle iron before I start to make the batter.

2 Once the iron is heated (not before), use a heat-resistant silicone brush or a pad of folded paper towels to grease the grids lightly with clarified butter. Be sure to cover the entire surface, especially if you are using a vintage iron with metal grids, but don't use so much butter that it pools in the hollows. Butter the grids even if you have a nonstick iron—the butter encourages a crisp, evenly browned waffle and adds extra flavor. In a pinch, you can use vegetable oil.

3 Waffle batter should never be overmixed. Gently stir or fold it just until the ingredients are combined. Don't worry if it is a bit lumpy; the lumps will eventually dissolve as you use the batter. As the batter stands, it may thicken; if necessary, stir in a little milk to return it to its original consistency.

4 The amount of batter your waffle iron takes depends on your model, because capacities vary—which also means that the yields may vary. For my standard round waffle iron, I scoop ½ cup batter into the center of the four quadrants. I like to use a 2½-inch-diameter ice-cream scoop to fill it and I've found that 1½ scoops of batter is the right amount. Experiment with yours to see how many scoops you need. Don't worry if a bit of batter oozes out the sides—that's part of the waffle-making experience. Just scrape it off once it sets.

5 Avoid overcooking the waffles. Some cookbooks suggest baking until the steam escaping from the batter subsides—that's a surefire path to overcooking. The only reliable method is to open the lid and take a peek. The waffles should be golden brown and crisp around the edges. But don't open the lid for at least 3 minutes, and when you do open the iron, go slowly, because if the waffle isn't done, it could tear apart.

6 Waffles are best served hot out of the iron, but they can be kept warm in a preheated 200°F oven for about 10 minutes. Place the waffles directly on an oven rack so air can circulate around them. Don't stack them, or they'll get soggy.

7 Be sure the accompaniments are also warm or at room temperature (with the exception, of course, of whipped cream). And warm the plates in the oven for a few minutes while you make the waffles.

8 You can freeze any leftover waffles for another meal. Place the cooled waffles in zip-tight freezer bags, separating the waffles with waxed paper, and freeze for up to 1 month. To reheat, place on parchment paper–lined half-sheet pans and warm in a preheated 350°F oven until heated through, about 10 minutes. They won't be quite as crisp as when freshly made, but they'll still be very good.

Yeasted Waffles
with Bacon Twists

Makes about 8 waffles; 4 to 6 servings

I find this buttery waffle to be pretty special. I like what happens to the texture of a yeast-raised waffle as it cooks, how it becomes crisp on the outside and especially airy inside. I really enjoy the fermented scent and taste of yeast in these waffles. The batter needs to sit overnight to develop that depth of flavor. These waffles are the ideal foundation for both sweet and salty toppings, which is why I serve them with bacon and maple syrup or sandwich them with a variety of fillings.

COOK'S NOTE: You need to prepare the yeasted base of the batter ahead and refrigerate it overnight. The next morning, add the eggs and baking soda just before baking the waffles.

1 tablespoon (14 grams) crumbled compressed fresh yeast or 1¾ teaspoons (5 grams) active dry yeast

2 tablespoons superfine sugar

2 cups (448 grams) whole milk, warmed

8 tablespoons (114 grams) unsalted butter, melted

2¼ cups (320 grams) unbleached all-purpose flour

½ teaspoon fine sea salt

2 large eggs

¼ teaspoon baking soda

Clarified Butter (page 54) or vegetable oil, for the waffle iron

Warm pure maple syrup, for serving

Bacon Twists (page 245), for serving

1 If using compressed yeast, in a large bowl, combine the yeast and sugar. Let stand until the yeast gives off some moisture, about 5 minutes, then whisk to dissolve the yeast. Whisk in the milk and then the butter until well combined. (Or, if using active dry yeast, in a large bowl, sprinkle the yeast over ¼ cup of the milk. Let stand until the yeast softens, about 5 minutes, then whisk to dissolve. Whisk in the sugar, butter, and the remaining 1¾ cups milk until well combined.)

2 In a medium bowl, whisk the flour and salt to combine. Gradually whisk into the milk mixture until well mixed. Cover tightly with plastic wrap and refrigerate overnight.

3 When ready to make the waffles, heat a waffle iron according to the manufacturer's directions.

4 Meanwhile, in a small bowl, whisk the eggs and baking soda. Pour over the waffle batter, then stir with a whisk until well mixed.

5 Lightly grease the waffle iron grids with clarified butter. Using a dry measuring cup or ice-cream scoop, place the correct amount of batter in the center of the iron's quadrants (page 77). Close the lid and bake until the waffle is crisp and golden brown, 4 to 6 minutes.

6 Transfer the waffle to a warmed serving plate and serve immediately, with warm syrup and bacon twists. Make and serve the remaining waffles.

Bacon, Lettuce, and Tomato Waffles: Bake the waffles, keeping them warm on the rack of a preheated 200°F oven. Spread the whole waffles with mayonnaise. For each sandwich, top one waffle with Baked Bacon (page 245) strips, Boston or Bibb lettuce leaves, and thin slices of ripe beefsteak tomato. Top with a second whole waffle, lining up the quadrant marks, to make a "sandwich." Cut the waffles into quarters and secure each one with a toothpick (photo page 79).

Smoked Salmon and Goat Cheese Waffles: Bake the waffles, keeping them warm on the rack of a preheated 200°F oven. Cut the waffles into quadrants. Spread each with some Goat Cheese Spread (page 171) and top with thin slices of smoked salmon and a sprinkling of snipped fresh chives.

Buttermilk Waffles
with Fresh Berries and Cream

Makes about 10 waffles; 6 to 8 servings

For old-fashioned farmhouse taste, these golden-brown waffles can't be beat. They deliver a cakey but delicate interior and a hint of tangy flavor. To serve them, you can go the classic route and offer maple syrup and butter, or get a little fancier with one of the berry sauces (page 168). Because they're not sweet, they also work well for savory combinations.

3 cups (426 grams) unbleached all-purpose flour

2 tablespoons superfine sugar

2 teaspoons baking powder

1 teaspoon baking soda

½ teaspoon fine sea salt

8 tablespoons (114 grams) unsalted butter, cut into ½-inch cubes and chilled

2 cups (448 grams) low-fat buttermilk

1 cup (224 grams) whole milk

2 large eggs

Clarified Butter (page 54) or vegetable oil, for the waffle iron

Softened unsalted butter, for serving

Warm pure maple syrup, for serving

Fresh berries, for serving

Whipped Cream (page 50), for serving

1 Heat a waffle iron according to the manufacturer's directions.

2 Meanwhile, in a food processor, pulse the flour, sugar, baking powder, baking soda, and salt to combine. Add the butter and pulse 15 to 20 times, until it is very finely chopped and the mixture resembles coarse meal. Transfer to a large bowl and make a well in the center. (Alternatively, in a large bowl, whisk the dry ingredients. Toss in the butter to coat with the flour mixture, then cut it in with a pastry blender or rub in with your fingertips until the mixture resembles coarse meal. Make a well in the center.)

3 In a medium bowl, whisk the buttermilk, milk, and eggs until combined. Pour into the well and fold with the whisk just until combined. Don't worry about lumps.

4 Lightly grease the waffle iron grids with clarified butter. Using a dry measuring cup or ice-cream scoop, place the correct amount of batter in the center of the iron's quadrants (page 77). Close the lid and bake until the waffle is crisp and golden brown, 4 to 6 minutes.

5 Transfer the waffle to a warmed serving plate and serve immediately, with softened butter, warm syrup, berries, and whipped cream passed on the side. Make and serve the remaining waffles.

Fresh Corn Waffles

Makes about 8 waffles; 4 to 6 servings

When summer corn is at its peak, this waffle is extraordinary. But truth be told, it is pretty good made with canned corn too. The kernels lend a little crunchy pop to each bite. Although corn adds a subtle natural sweetness to these waffles, they work just as well as an accompaniment to a savory meal.

2½ cups (355 grams) unbleached all-purpose flour

3 tablespoons superfine sugar

2 teaspoons baking powder

½ teaspoon fine sea salt

1⅔ cups (373 grams) whole milk

2 large eggs

½ teaspoon pure vanilla extract

3 tablespoons unsalted butter, melted and cooled, or vegetable oil

2½ cups (395 grams) fresh corn kernels (cut from 3 or 4 ears)

Clarified Butter (page 54) or vegetable oil, for the waffle iron

Warm pure maple syrup or honey, for serving

Crème fraîche or yogurt, for serving

Seasonal fresh fruit, for serving

1 Heat a waffle iron according the manufacturer's directions.

2 In a large bowl, whisk the flour, sugar, baking powder, and salt. Make a well in the center. In a medium bowl, whisk the milk, eggs, vanilla, and melted butter. Pour into the well and fold with the whisk just until the batter is combined. Don't worry about lumps. Fold in the corn until the batter is completely mixed.

3 Lightly grease the waffle iron grids with clarified butter. Using a dry measuring cup or ice-cream scoop, place the correct amount of batter in the center of the iron's quadrants (page 77). Close the lid and bake until the waffle is crisp and golden brown, 4 to 6 minutes.

4 Transfer the waffle to a warmed serving plate and serve immediately, with warm syrup, crème fraîche, and fruit passed on the side. Make and serve the remaining waffles.

Gingerbread-Coffee Waffles

Makes about 8 waffles; 4 to 6 servings

These gently spiced waffles are just the thing for a special holiday brunch—and they will turn an ordinary morning meal into a festive one. The coffee complements the warm spices perfectly, both in taste and the mouthwatering fragrance of the baking waffles. For a little more spice, increase the ground ginger to 1 teaspoon.

3 cups (426 grams) unbleached all-purpose flour
¼ cup (49 grams) packed light brown sugar
2 teaspoons baking powder
½ teaspoon baking soda
1 teaspoon ground cinnamon
½ teaspoon ground ginger
¼ teaspoon ground cloves
½ teaspoon fine sea salt
6 tablespoons (85 grams) unsalted butter, cut into ½-inch cubes and chilled
⅓ cup (54 grams) crystallized ginger, finely chopped
1¼ cups (280 grams) whole milk
¾ cup (168 grams) strong brewed coffee
2 large eggs
Clarified Butter (page 54) or vegetable oil, for the waffle iron
Softened unsalted butter, for serving
Warm pure maple syrup, for serving

1 Heat a waffle iron according to the manufacturer's directions.

2 Meanwhile, in a food processor, pulse the flour, brown sugar, baking powder, baking soda, cinnamon, ground ginger, cloves, and salt to combine. Add the butter and pulse 15 to 20 times, until it is very finely chopped and the mixture resembles coarse meal. Transfer to a bowl and toss in the crystallized ginger. Make a well in the center. (Alternatively, whisk the dry ingredients in a large bowl. Toss in the butter to coat with the flour mixture, then cut it in with a pastry blender or rub in with your fingertips until the mixture resembles coarse meal. Toss in the crystallized ginger. Make a well in the center.)

3 In a medium bowl, whisk the milk, coffee, and eggs until combined. Pour into the well and fold with the whisk just until the batter is combined. Don't worry about lumps.

4 Lightly grease the waffle iron grids with clarified butter. Using a dry measuring cup or ice-cream scoop, place the correct amount of batter in the center of the iron's quadrants (page 77). Close the lid and bake until the waffle is crisp and golden brown, 4 to 6 minutes.

5 Transfer the waffle to a warmed serving plate and serve immediately, with softened butter and warm syrup passed on the side. Make and serve the remaining waffles.

Pumpkin Waffles
with Sour Cream and Toasted Pumpkin Seeds

Makes about 6 waffles; 4 to 6 servings

One morning at my original restaurant, I was feeling adventurous during breakfast service. While we were scooping the pumpkin muffin batter into the tins, I also baked off a scoop in the waffle iron. I took a bite and thought, "This is really good." I wasn't the only one who thought so. Once I perfected my pumpkin waffles and started serving them, they immediately became one of our signature waffles. Customers have patiently waited in long lines just to eat them. Slightly sweet and accented with warm spices, this waffle is fantastic with a dollop of sour cream and a sprinkle of crunchy toasted pumpkin seeds. Raisins add a little extra sweetness, but some people prefer these with a bit of honey instead.

2 cups (284 grams) unbleached all-purpose flour
⅓ cup (65 grams) superfine sugar
2 teaspoons baking powder
½ teaspoon ground cinnamon
¼ teaspoon ground ginger
⅛ teaspoon freshly grated nutmeg
½ teaspoon fine sea salt
6 tablespoons (85 grams) unsalted butter, cut into ½-inch cubes and chilled
½ cup (112 grams) whole milk
½ cup (116 grams) heavy cream
⅓ cup (93 grams) unsweetened solid-pack pumpkin
3 large eggs
Seeds from 1 vanilla bean, preferably a Plumped Vanilla Bean (page 3), or 1 teaspoon pure vanilla extract
Clarified Butter (page 54) or vegetable oil, for the waffle iron
Warm pure maple syrup, for serving
Sour cream, at room temperature, for serving
Pepitas (hulled pumpkin seeds), toasted (page 41), for garnish
Raisins, for garnish

1 Heat a waffle iron according to the manufacturer's directions.

2 Meanwhile, in a food processor, pulse the flour, sugar, baking powder, cinnamon, ginger, nutmeg, and salt to combine. Add the butter and pulse 15 to 20 times, until it is very finely chopped and the mixture resembles coarse meal. Transfer to a bowl and make a well in the center. (Alternatively, whisk the dry ingredients in a large bowl. Toss in the butter to coat with the flour mixture, then cut it in with a pastry blender or rub in with your fingertips until the mixture resembles coarse meal. Make a well in the center.)

3 In a medium bowl, whisk the milk, cream, pumpkin, eggs, and vanilla until combined. Pour into the well and fold with the whisk just until the batter is combined. Don't worry about lumps.

4 Lightly grease the waffle iron grids with clarified butter. Using a dry measuring cup or ice-cream scoop, place the correct amount of batter in the center of the iron's quadrants (page 77). Close the lid and bake until the waffle is crisp and golden brown, 4 to 6 minutes.

5 Transfer the waffle to a warmed serving plate and serve immediately, with the warm syrup, sour cream, pumpkin seeds, and raisins passed on the side. Make and serve the remaining waffles.

Lemon-Almond Waffles
with Amaretto Maple Syrup

Makes about 8 waffles; 4 to 6 servings

This crisp waffle gets its delightful texture from the heavy cream and amaretto in the batter. Amaretto makes another appearance in the syrup, where it accentuates the almond scent of the hot-off-the-iron waffles. They bake up more quickly than the other waffles in this book, so keep an eye on them as they cook.

1 cup (292 grams) pure maple syrup, warmed

¼ cup (56 grams) plus 2 tablespoons amaretto

3 cups (426 grams) unbleached all-purpose flour

¼ cup (49 grams) superfine sugar

1 tablespoon baking powder

1 teaspoon packed freshly grated lemon zest

½ teaspoon fine sea salt

6 tablespoons (85 grams) unsalted butter, cut into ½-inch cubes and chilled

1½ cups (336 grams) whole milk

½ cup (116 grams) heavy cream

2 large eggs

Clarified Butter (page 54) or vegetable oil, for the waffle iron

1 Heat a waffle iron according to the manufacturer's directions.

2 In a small bowl, stir together the maple syrup and 2 tablespoons amaretto. Reserve for serving.

3 Meanwhile, in a food processor, pulse the flour, sugar, baking powder, lemon zest, and salt to combine. Add the butter and pulse 15 to 20 times, until it is very finely chopped and the mixture resembles coarse meal. Transfer to a bowl and make a well in the center. (Alternatively, whisk the dry ingredients and the lemon zest in a large bowl. Toss in the butter to coat with the flour mixture, then cut it in with a pastry blender or rub in with your fingertips until the mixture resembles coarse meal. Make a well in the center.)

4 In a medium bowl, whisk the milk, cream, eggs, and the remaining ¼ cup amaretto until combined. Pour into the well and fold with the whisk just until the batter is combined. Don't worry about lumps.

5 Lightly grease the waffle iron grids with clarified butter. Using a dry measuring cup or ice-cream scoop, place the correct amount of batter in the center of the iron's quadrants (page 77). Close the lid and bake until the waffle is crisp and golden brown, 3 to 4 minutes.

6 Transfer the waffle to a warmed serving plate and serve immediately, with the amaretto syrup passed on the side. Make and serve the remaining waffles.

Fat-and-Fluffy French Toast

Makes 4 to 8 servings

Soft and custardy on the inside, crisp and buttery on the outside, this is French toast heaven. A quick trip to the oven gives the sautéed French toast extra lightness. I use challah, a golden braided bread from the Jewish baking tradition. Other egg-rich breads, such as brioche or Greek egg bread, are also perfect—see what your bakery has that will fit the bill. Serve with maple syrup and butter or a fresh berry sauce (page 168).

12 large eggs

1½ cups (336 grams) whole milk

1 tablespoon superfine sugar

1 teaspoon pure vanilla extract

Pinch of freshly grated nutmeg

1 large loaf (18 ounces; 510 grams) egg bread, such as a Challah Loaf (page 145), cut into eight 1-inch-thick slices (on the diagonal if using a braided challah), then cut diagonally in half

Clarified Butter (page 54), as needed

Confectioners' sugar, for garnish

Warm pure maple syrup, for serving

Softened unsalted butter, for serving

1 Position a rack in the center of the oven and preheat to 350°F. Thoroughly heat a griddle or a large skillet over medium heat.

2 In a medium bowl, whisk the eggs, milk, superfine sugar, vanilla, and nutmeg. Strain through a fine-mesh sieve into a shallow bowl.

3 Pierce the bread slices all over with a fork. Add a few bread slices to the egg mixture and turn until evenly soaked.

4 Brush the griddle or skillet with clarified butter. Add the slices of bread in a single layer, spacing them 1 inch apart, and cook until the undersides are golden brown, about 3 minutes. Turn and cook until the other sides are golden, 2 to 3 more minutes. Stand each piece of French toast on its cut side and cook for 1 minute. Transfer to a parchment paper–lined half-sheet pan. Repeat with the remaining bread and egg mixture.

5 Bake the French toast until slightly puffed and cooked through, 7 to 10 minutes. Serve immediately on warmed plates, dusted with confectioners' sugar, passing warm syrup and softened butter on the side.

Almond French Toast with Raspberries: Toast 1 cup (116 grams) sliced almonds (page 41). Add 1 teaspoon pure almond extract to the egg mixture. Make the French toast as directed, but generously sprinkle each serving with almonds and fresh raspberries before serving (photo opposite).

Strawberries-and-Cream French Toast: Spread a slice of French toast with a generous layer of Strawberry-Rhubarb Preserves (page 175). Top with another slice of French toast. Crown with a dollop of Whipped Cream (page 50) and sliced strawberries.

Apple-Cinnamon French Toast: Use Apple-Cinnamon Bread (page 143). Serve with warm Apple Maple Syrup (page 167) or Chunky Apple Butter (page 181). Top with raisins and sliced bananas.

Cheesecake-Stuffed French Toast with Orange Drizzle: Mix 8 ounces (227 grams) softened farmer cheese, 8 ounces (227 grams) softened cream cheese, 2 tablespoons superfine sugar, and ½ teaspoon freshly grated lemon zest with a silicone spatula until well blended. Spread on half the baked French toast slices and top with the remaining slices. Return to the oven to heat through, about 5 minutes. Meanwhile, blend 1 cup (308 grams) Mandarin Orange Spread (page 176), ⅓ cup (75 grams) fresh orange juice, 1 teaspoon pure vanilla extract, and 2 teaspoons fresh lemon juice. Drizzle over the French toast.

Apple Cider French Toast
with Streusel

Makes 8 servings

Apple cider gives this French toast a gentle tang, and the streusel adds a touch of sweetness. This works well with any nice, tender white bread, but it is especially good made with my Great Bread. While the streusel-crusted slices taste fabulous alone, they're even better with bacon or sausages on the side.

Streusel

1 cup (142 grams) unbleached all-purpose flour

2 tablespoons packed light brown sugar

2 tablespoons superfine sugar

¾ teaspoon ground cinnamon

⅛ teaspoon freshly grated nutmeg

4 tablespoons (57 grams) unsalted butter, melted and cooled

½ teaspoon pure vanilla extract

12 large eggs

1½ cups (336 grams) fresh apple cider

1 teaspoon pure vanilla extract

⅛ teaspoon freshly grated nutmeg

1 large loaf (18 ounces; 510 grams) Great Bread (page 138) or other tender white bread, cut into eight 1-inch-thick slices, then cut diagonally in half

Clarified Butter (page 54), as needed

Softened unsalted butter, for serving

Warm pure maple syrup, for serving

Sliced bananas, for serving

Blueberries, for serving

Walnuts, toasted (page 41) and chopped, for serving, optional

1 Position a rack in the center of the oven and preheat to 350°F. Thoroughly heat a griddle or a large skillet over medium heat.

2 To make the streusel: Whisk the flour, brown sugar, superfine sugar, cinnamon, and nutmeg in a medium bowl. Mix in the butter and vanilla with your fingertips until combined and crumbly. Transfer to a shallow baking dish.

3 To make the French toast: In a medium bowl, whisk the eggs, cider, vanilla, and nutmeg. Pour through a fine-mesh sieve into a shallow bowl.

4 Pierce the bread slices all over with a fork. Add a few bread slices to the egg mixture and turn until evenly soaked. Transfer to the dish with the streusel and coat both sides of each slice, patting to help the streusel adhere.

5 Brush the griddle or skillet with clarified butter. Add the slices of bread in a single layer, spacing them 1 inch

apart, and cook until the undersides are golden brown, about 3 minutes. Turn and cook until the other sides are golden, 2 to 3 more minutes. Stand each piece of French toast on its cut side and cook for 1 minute. Transfer to a parchment paper–lined half-sheet pan. Repeat with the remaining bread, egg mixture, and streusel.

6 Bake the French toast until slightly puffed and cooked through, 7 to 10 minutes. Serve immediately on warmed plates, passing softened butter, warm syrup, bananas, blueberries, and walnuts, if using, on the side.

Whole-Grain French Toast
with Sautéed Bananas

Makes 8 servings

Caramelized bananas elevate any French toast, but they pair especially well with Sarabeth's House Bread, which is packed with whole grains and seeds. (Any hearty, nutty loaf will have enough heft for buttery bananas.) Together, they make a satisfying breakfast that will fuel you through even your busiest day.

12 large eggs

1½ cups (336 grams) whole milk

2 tablespoons pure maple syrup

1 teaspoon pure vanilla extract

1 large loaf (18 ounces; 510 grams) Sarabeth's House Bread (page 140) or other hearty whole-grain loaf, cut into eight 1-inch-thick slices, then cut diagonally in half

Clarified Butter (page 54), as needed

4 large ripe but firm bananas, cut into ½-inch-thick slices

2 tablespoons Demerara sugar

2 tablespoons unsalted butter

1 Position a rack in the center of the oven and preheat to 350°F. Thoroughly heat a griddle or a large skillet over medium heat.

2 In a medium bowl, whisk the eggs, milk, syrup, and vanilla. Pour through a fine-mesh sieve into a shallow bowl.

3 Pierce the bread slices all over with a fork. Add a few bread slices to the egg mixture and turn until evenly soaked.

4 Brush the griddle or skillet with clarified butter. Add the slices of bread in a single layer, spacing them 1 inch apart, and cook until the undersides are golden brown, about 3 minutes. Turn and cook until the other sides are golden, 2 to 3 more minutes. Stand each piece of French toast on its cut side and cook for 1 minute. Transfer to a parchment paper–lined half-sheet pan. Repeat with the remaining bread.

5 Bake the French toast until slightly puffed and cooked through, 7 to 10 minutes.

6 Meanwhile, in a large bowl, toss the bananas with the Demerara sugar. Melt the 2 tablespoons butter in a large skillet over medium heat. Add the bananas and cook, gently stirring, until they are caramelized and browned, about 5 minutes.

7 Serve the French toast immediately on warmed plates, topped with the bananas.

PINT
20oz
2 CUPS
16oz
12oz
8oz

Chapter Five

Muffins, Scones, and Cakes

I BELIEVE IN CAKE FOR BREAKFAST, WHETHER IT COMES IN THE FORM OF AN ACTUAL CAKE OR CAKE DISGUISED AS MUFFINS OR SCONES. LARGE, TENDER cakes are ideal make-ahead treats for brunches and parties, and muffins and scones bake quickly enough for any morning. All share a measured sweetness that satisfies without causing a sugar high.

When I bake for breakfast, I still use my baker's instincts. In this chapter, you'll find helpful tips on how to make exceptional creations. I cream the butter for muffins, use a light touch with scones, and mix cake batters carefully. The results taste like luxurious four-star desserts you can justify enjoying first thing in the morning.

TOOL KIT

Muffin Pans: I use heavy muffin tins with cups that are 2 ¾ inches across and 1½ inches deep, with a 7-tablespoon capacity. Different pans may have varying cup sizes, so figure out the volume of yours by counting the number of tablespoons it takes to fill a cup to the brim with water. If necessary, adjust the amount of batter you place in each cup. Don't use a pan with a dark finish; it will make your muffins too brown.

Biscuit Cutters: To cleanly cut scones, biscuits, and shortcakes, use sturdy round cutters with smooth or fluted edges. I have a professional set made from white composite plastic, which cut more cleanly than metal cutters, but the latter work fine too.

Fluted Cake Pans: Bundt cakes look beautiful on the breakfast table. I use heavy cast-metal 10- and 12-cup-capacity pans. Avoid dark-colored pans, even if they have a nonstick interior—dark pans absorb more heat in the oven and will make the outside of the cake too brown. A properly buttered and floured pan works just as well as a nonstick one. If you must use a nonstick pan, preheat the oven to the temperature specified, but reduce the temperature by 25°F once the cake is in the oven, and watch carefully for doneness.

Ice-Cream Scoop: A 2½-inch-diameter scoop is the best tool for evenly portioning muffin and cake batters and scone dough.

Cake Tester: To test for doneness, use a thin wire cake tester which won't leave a hole the way a toothpick or skewer will.

TIPS FOR PERFECT MUFFINS

1 Skip paper liners—butter the muffin pan instead. Be sure to use well-softened butter and a round brush with natural bristles. (In a pinch, you can use a folded paper towel.) Thoroughly butter the cups and the top of the pan—by greasing the areas between the cups, you can ensure that not even a crumb will stick.

2 Use chilled butter to make the batter so that your muffins will have domed tops. The butter should be quite cool but malleable before being beaten. To make sure that the batter ends up evenly mixed, stop the machine occasionally and scrape down the bottom and sides of the bowl.

3 Another way to guarantee that picture-perfect dome is to portion the batter with an ice-cream scoop. It also eliminates mess and makes all of the muffins the same size. I use a 2½-inch-diameter ice-cream scoop with a generous ⅓-cup capacity. When I release the batter, I center the mound in the cup to create a symmetrical top.

4 If the recipe makes more than a dozen muffins, divide the batter evenly between two pans. For example, if you are making 18 muffins, bake 9 in each pan.

5 Cool the muffins in the pan for 10 minutes to make sure they hold their shape, then immediately unmold. Leave them any longer, and they'll steam and get soggy bottoms. You don't need to finish cooling them on a wire rack—a sheet of parchment paper will do—but you can use one if you'd like. Just be sure to eat the muffins the same day they're baked.

Nectarine-Blueberry Crumb Muffins

Makes 16 muffins

Just when I thought I couldn't give my classic blueberry muffins a more delicate crumb, I did. Thick Greek yogurt and juicy nectarines bring another level of tenderness to the buttery blueberry base. Plus, those additions deliver great flavor—so does my signature streusel topping.

Streusel

½ cup (71 grams) unbleached all-purpose flour

1 tablespoon plus 1 teaspoon superfine sugar

1 tablespoon plus 1 teaspoon packed light brown sugar

¼ teaspoon ground cinnamon

⅛ teaspoon fine sea salt

½ teaspoon pure vanilla extract

3 tablespoons unsalted butter, melted and cooled

Softened unsalted butter, for the pans

3½ cups (497 grams) unbleached all-purpose flour

2 teaspoons baking powder

1 teaspoon baking soda

½ teaspoon fine sea salt

2 teaspoons pure vanilla extract

¾ cup (147 grams) superfine sugar

¾ cup (147 grams) packed light brown sugar

12 tablespoons (171 grams) unsalted butter, chilled and cut into ½-inch cubes

3 large eggs, at room temperature, beaten

1 cup (234 grams) fat-free Greek yogurt

1½ cups (235 grams) chopped nectarines (about 2 medium)

1 cup (142 grams) blueberries

1 Position a rack in the center of the oven and preheat to 400°F. Brush the insides of 16 muffin cups with softened butter, then brush the tops of the pans.

2 To make the streusel: In a small bowl, mix the flour, superfine sugar, brown sugar, cinnamon, salt, vanilla, and butter with your fingers until combined and crumbly. Set aside.

3 In a medium bowl, whisk the flour, baking powder, baking soda, and salt. In a small bowl, rub the vanilla into the superfine and brown sugars with your fingertips.

4 In the bowl of a heavy-duty stand mixer fitted with the paddle attachment, beat the butter on high speed until smooth, about 1 minute. Scrape the sides of the bowl with a silicone spatula. Turn the mixer speed to medium-high. Gradually add the sugar mixture and continue beating, scraping the sides of the bowl often with a silicone spatula, until the mixture is very light in color and texture, about 5 minutes. Gradually beat in the eggs.

5 Reduce the mixer speed to low. In thirds, add the flour mixture, alternating with two additions of the yogurt, scraping the sides of the bowl and beating briefly after each addition; do not overbeat. Fold in the nectarines and blueberries.

6 Using a 2½-inch-diameter ice-cream scoop, portion the batter, rounded side up, into the prepared muffin cups. Squeeze handfuls of the streusel mixture, then break into small clumps and generously sprinkle the tops of the muffins with the streusel clumps and crumbs.

7 Bake for 10 minutes. Reduce the oven temperature to 375°F and bake until the muffin tops are golden brown and a cake tester inserted into the center of a muffin comes out clean, about 15 minutes longer.

8 Cool in the pans for 10 minutes. Remove the muffins from the pans and cool completely.

Poppy Seed Muffins

Makes 16 muffins

Cream cheese gives these sunny yellow muffins a texture almost like pound cake. (In fact, you can bake these in mini loaf pans if you'd like.) There's just a hint of lemon here so that the flavor of the poppy seeds can really shine. If you're not starting with a fresh jar of poppy seeds (or even if you are), be sure to sniff them first, as poppy seeds tend to go rancid quickly.

Softened unsalted butter, for the pans

2¼ cups (320 grams) unbleached all-purpose flour

¼ cup (39 grams) poppy seeds

2 teaspoons baking powder

½ teaspoon fine sea salt

1 teaspoon freshly grated lemon zest

2 teaspoons pure vanilla extract

1⅓ cups (261 grams) superfine sugar

1 cup (227 grams) unsalted butter, chilled and cut into ½-inch cubes

8 ounces (227 grams) cream cheese, at room temperature

4 large eggs, at room temperature, beaten

1 Position a rack in the center of the oven and preheat to 400°F. Brush the insides of 16 muffin cups with softened butter, then brush the tops of the pans.

2 In a medium bowl, whisk the flour, poppy seeds, baking powder, and salt. In a small bowl, rub the lemon zest and vanilla into the sugar with your fingertips.

3 In the bowl of a heavy-duty stand mixer fitted with the paddle attachment, beat the butter on high speed until smooth, about 1 minute. Scrape the sides of the bowl with a silicone spatula. Add the cream cheese and beat on medium speed until smooth and fluffy, with the consistency of buttercream, about 5 minutes. Gradually add the sugar mixture and continue beating, scraping the sides of the bowl often, until the mixture is very light in color and texture, about 5 minutes. Gradually beat in the eggs.

4 Scrape the sides of the bowl and turn the mixer speed to low. Gradually add the flour mixture and beat just until combined. Scrape the bowl, then beat on medium-high speed for 10 seconds, to ensure everything is well mixed.

5 Using a 2½-inch-diameter ice-cream scoop, portion the batter, rounded side up, into the prepared muffin cups.

6 Bake for 10 minutes. Reduce the oven temperature to 375°F and bake until the muffin tops are golden brown and a cake tester inserted into the center of a muffin comes out clean, about 15 minutes longer.

7 Cool in the pans for 10 minutes. Remove the muffins from the pans and cool completely.

Low-Fat Raspberry Muffins

Makes 1 dozen muffins

For a nice, healthy alternative to fluffy, buttery muffins, try these hearty bran ones. They're very moist and grainy, and I love them. Pumpkin is a great replacement for fat as it keeps the muffins moist. Also, it adds an earthy sweetness while raspberries provide a tangy zing. If you can't find small raspberries, cut large ones in half. Otherwise, you'll end up with large wet pockets in the baked muffins.

Softened unsalted butter, for the pan

2 cups (120 grams) wheat bran (not bran breakfast cereal)

1⅓ cups (189 grams) unbleached all-purpose flour

2 teaspoons baking powder

½ teaspoon fine sea salt

⅓ cup (65 grams) packed light brown sugar

⅓ cup (65 grams) superfine sugar

2 large eggs, at room temperature, beaten

1⅓ cups (299 grams) 2% reduced-fat milk

1 cup (279 grams) unsweetened solid-pack pumpkin

1 cup (95 grams) small raspberries

1 Position a rack in the center of the oven and preheat to 400°F. Brush the insides of 12 muffin cups with softened butter, then brush the top of the pan.

2 In a large bowl, whisk the bran, flour, baking powder, and salt. In another large bowl, whisk the brown and superfine sugars and the eggs until well blended, then whisk in the milk until smooth. Whisk in the pumpkin until incorporated.

3 Make a well in the dry ingredients. Pour in the wet ingredients and fold gently with a silicone spatula just until combined. Let the batter stand for 5 minutes, then fold in the raspberries.

4 Using a 2½-inch-diameter ice-cream scoop, portion the batter, rounded side up, into the prepared muffin cups.

5 Bake for 10 minutes. Reduce the oven temperature to 350°F and bake until the muffin tops are golden brown and a cake tester inserted into the center of a muffin comes out clean, about 25 minutes longer.

6 Cool in the pan for 10 minutes. Remove the muffins from the pan and cool completely.

Olive Oil-Ginger Muffins

Makes 1 dozen muffins

Olive oil gives these gingery muffins a nice little nip. I like using a subtle, fruity olive oil, such as Spanish Arbequina, which complements the aroma of the orange blossom water. Although there isn't any creamed butter in the recipe, the muffins are very moist and fluffy.

Softened unsalted butter, for the pan

2½ cups (355 grams) all-purpose flour

1 cup (196 grams) superfine sugar

1 tablespoon baking powder

¼ teaspoon fine sea salt

¼ cup (43 grams) finely chopped crystallized ginger, plus slivers for garnish

2 large eggs

1 cup (224 grams) whole milk

½ cup (110 grams) extra-virgin olive oil

½ teaspoon orange blossom water

1 Position a rack in the center of the oven and preheat to 400°F. Brush the insides of 12 muffin cups with softened butter, then brush the top of the pan.

2 In a large bowl, whisk the flour, sugar, baking powder, and salt. Add the chopped crystallized ginger and toss until evenly coated. In a medium bowl, whisk the eggs, milk, oil, and orange blossom water until smooth and well combined.

3 Make a well in the dry ingredients. Pour in the wet ingredients and fold gently with a silicone spatula just until combined.

4 Using a 2½-inch-diameter ice-cream scoop, portion the batter, rounded side up, into the prepared muffin cups. Top with crystallized ginger slivers.

5 Bake for 10 minutes. Reduce the oven temperature to 350°F and bake until the muffin tops are golden brown and a cake tester inserted into the center of a muffin comes out clean, about 10 minutes longer.

6 Cool in the pan for 10 minutes. Remove the muffins from the pan and cool completely.

Apple-Hazelnut Muffins

Makes 1½ dozen muffins

Hazelnuts are among my favorite nuts. Here they're both finely ground to enrich the apple-studded batter and coarsely chopped for a crunchy topping. Oats enhance the nuttiness of this fantastic fall muffin.

Softened unsalted butter, for the pans

1¼ cups (183 grams) hazelnuts, toasted and skinned (page 41)

2¼ cups (320 grams) all-purpose flour

1 cup (103 grams) old-fashioned rolled oats

2½ teaspoons baking powder

¾ teaspoon ground cinnamon

½ teaspoon fine sea salt

2 teaspoons pure vanilla extract

1⅓ cups (261 grams) superfine sugar

1 cup (227 grams) unsalted butter, chilled and cut into ½-inch cubes

2 large eggs, at room temperature, beaten

1 cup (224 grams) whole milk

2 cups (364 grams) ¼-inch-diced peeled Granny Smith apples (about 2 medium)

1 Position a rack in the center of the oven and preheat to 400°F. Brush the insides of 18 muffin cups with softened butter, then brush the tops of the pans.

2 In a food processor, pulse ¾ cup hazelnuts and ¼ cup flour until the nuts are finely ground. Add the oats and pulse until they are finely chopped. Transfer to a large bowl and whisk in the baking powder, cinnamon, salt, and the remaining 2 cups flour. In a small bowl, rub the vanilla into the sugar with your fingertips. Coarsely chop the remaining ½ cup hazelnuts and set aside.

3 In the bowl of a heavy-duty stand mixer fitted with the paddle attachment, beat the butter on high speed until smooth, about 1 minute. Gradually add the sugar mixture and continue beating, scraping the sides of the bowl often with a silicone spatula, until the mixture is very light in color and texture, about 5 minutes. Gradually beat in the eggs.

4 Reduce the mixer speed to low. In thirds, add the flour mixture, alternating with two additions of the milk, scraping the sides of the bowl and beating briefly after each addition; do not overbeat. Fold in the apples.

5 Using a 2½-inch-diameter ice-cream scoop, portion the batter, rounded side up, into the prepared muffin cups. Sprinkle the tops with the reserved chopped hazelnuts.

6 Bake for 10 minutes. Reduce the oven temperature to 375°F and bake until the muffin tops are golden brown and a cake tester inserted into the center of a muffin comes out clean, about 15 minutes longer.

7 Cool in the pans for 10 minutes. Remove the muffins from the pans and cool completely.

TIPS FOR PERFECT SCONES, BISCUITS, AND SHORTCAKES

1 The key to tender scones, biscuits, and shortcakes is to avoid overhandling the dough, which would activate the gluten in the flour and make the pastries tough.

2 Always use well-chilled butter that has been cut into small ½-inch cubes. This will create flecks of butter in the dough that melt when baking—leaving air pockets that make for light and fluffy baked goods.

3 When you need to cut the dough into rounds, be sure your cutters are good and sharp—dull edges compress the sides and prevent a good rise.

Cranberry Cream Scones

Makes 16 scones

To make morning baking especially fast for busy home cooks, I adapted my classic scones into these easy drop scones. There's no kneading, rolling, or cutting involved. All you need is an ice-cream scoop to drop the cranberry batter onto the pan. The generous amount of cream makes these cranberry scones wonderfully tender and tasty.

1¼ cups (290 grams) heavy cream

2 large cold eggs

3 cups (426 grams) unbleached all-purpose flour

1 tablespoon baking powder

3 tablespoons superfine sugar

½ teaspoon fine sea salt

8 tablespoons (114 grams) unsalted butter, cut into ½-inch cubes and chilled

¾ cup (120 grams) dried cranberries

1 Position a rack in the center of the oven and preheat to 425°F. Line a half-sheet pan with parchment paper.

2 TO MAKE THE DOUGH BY HAND: In a small bowl, whisk the cream and eggs; set aside. In a medium bowl, whisk the flour, baking powder, sugar, and salt. Add the butter and toss to coat it with the flour mixture. Using a pastry blender, cut the butter into the flour, scraping the butter off the blender as needed, until the mixture resembles coarse bread crumbs with some pea-sized pieces of butter. Mix in the cranberries. Using a wooden spoon, stir in the cream mixture and mix just until the dough clumps together. TO MAKE THE DOUGH WITH A MIXER: In a small bowl, whisk the cream and eggs; set aside. In the bowl of a heavy-duty stand mixer, whisk the dry ingredients. Toss in the butter. Attach the bowl to the mixer and fit the mixer with the paddle attachment. Mix on medium-low speed until the mixture looks mealy with some pea-sized bits of butter. Mix in the cranberries. Reduce the mixer speed to low and add the cream mixture, mixing just until the dough comes together.

3 Using a 2½-inch-diameter ice-cream scoop, portion the dough, rounded side up, onto the prepared half-sheet pan, spacing the scones 1½ inches apart.

4 Place the scones in the oven and immediately reduce the heat to 400°F. Bake until golden brown, 15 to 20 minutes. Cool on the pan for a few minutes and serve warm, or let cool completely.

Earl Grey Scones

Makes 16 scones

Since we opened Sarabeth's restaurants and bakeries in Japan, I've returned from each trip there with fresh ideas. This was one of them. Earl Grey tea leaves are both steeped in the cream and ground and mixed into the dough so you can really taste the aromatic bergamot notes in these sophisticated morning—or afternoon—treats. They bring a whole new meaning to tea scones.

BAKER'S NOTE: The tea leaves need to be steeped in the cream for at least 8 hours, or overnight.

1¼ cups (290 grams) heavy cream, plus more as needed

2 tablespoons plus 4 teaspoons Earl Grey tea leaves

2 large cold eggs

3 cups (426 grams) unbleached all-purpose flour

1 tablespoon baking powder

¼ cup (49 grams) superfine sugar

½ teaspoon fine sea salt

8 tablespoons (114 grams) unsalted butter, cut into ½-inch cubes and chilled

2 tablespoons turbinado sugar, for sprinkling

1 In a small bowl, stir the cream and 2 tablespoons tea leaves together. Cover and refrigerate for at least 8 hours, or up to overnight.

2 When ready to bake, position a rack in the center of the oven and preheat to 425°F. Line a half-sheet pan with parchment paper.

3 Finely grind the remaining 4 teaspoons tea leaves in a spice grinder. Set aside.

4 Strain the cream mixture through a fine-mesh sieve into a large liquid measuring cup, pressing on the tea leaves to extract as much liquid as possible. Discard the tea leaves. Add more cream as needed to make 1¼ cups. Whisk the eggs into the cream; set aside.

5 TO MAKE THE DOUGH BY HAND: In a medium bowl, whisk the flour, baking powder, superfine sugar, salt, and ground tea leaves. Add the butter and toss to coat it with the flour mixture. Using a pastry blender, cut the butter into the flour, scraping the butter off the blender as needed, until the mixture resembles coarse bread crumbs with some pea-sized pieces of butter. Using a wooden spoon, stir in the cream mixture and mix just until the dough clumps together. TO MAKE THE DOUGH WITH A MIXER: In the bowl of a heavy-duty stand mixer, whisk the dry ingredients. Toss in the butter. Attach the bowl to the mixer and fit the mixer with the paddle attachment. Mix on medium-low speed until the mixture looks mealy with some pea-sized bits of butter. Reduce the mixer speed to low and add the cream mixture, mixing just until the dough comes together.

6 Using a 2½-inch-diameter ice-cream scoop, portion the dough, rounded side up, onto the prepared half-sheet pan, spacing the scones 1½ inches apart. Sprinkle the tops with the turbinado sugar.

7 Place the scones in the oven and immediately reduce the heat to 400°F. Bake until lightly browned, 15 to 20 minutes. Cool on the pan for a few minutes and serve warm, or let cool completely.

Whole Wheat Ginger Scones

Makes 16 scones

I created these scones out of a desire to use more whole grains in my baking and to find another ideal accompaniment to my many spreads. The nutty, earthy flavor of the whole wheat and the sweet bite of the crystallized ginger are just right with homemade spreads. Vanilla provides an added burst of flavor that makes these extra special.

1 cup (224 grams) whole milk

Seeds from ½ vanilla bean, preferably a Plumped Vanilla Bean (page 3), or ½ teaspoon pure vanilla extract

3 large cold eggs

1½ cups (213 grams) unbleached all-purpose flour, plus more as needed

1½ cups (225 grams) stone-ground whole wheat flour

1 tablespoon plus 1 teaspoon baking powder

3 tablespoons superfine sugar

½ teaspoon fine sea salt

¼ teaspoon ground cinnamon

10 tablespoons (142 grams) unsalted butter, cut into ½-inch cubes and chilled

⅓ cup (54 grams) crystallized ginger, cut into ¼-inch pieces

1 Position a rack in the center of the oven and preheat to 425°F. Line a half-sheet pan with parchment paper.

2 TO MAKE THE DOUGH BY HAND: In a small bowl, whisk the milk, vanilla seeds, and 2 eggs; set aside. Sift the all-purpose flour, whole wheat flour, baking powder, sugar, salt, and cinnamon into a medium bowl. Add the butter and toss to coat the butter with the flour mixture. Using a pastry blender, cut the butter into the flour, scraping the butter off the blender as needed, until the mixture resembles coarse bread crumbs with some pea-sized pieces of butter. Mix in the ginger. Using a wooden spoon, stir in the milk mixture and mix just until the dough clumps together. TO MAKE THE DOUGH WITH A MIXER: In a small bowl, whisk the milk, vanilla seeds, and 2 eggs; set aside. Sift the dry ingredients into the bowl of a heavy-duty stand mixer. Toss in the butter. Attach the bowl to the mixer and fit the mixer with the paddle attachment. Mix on medium-low speed until the mixture looks mealy with some pea-sized bits of butter. Mix in the ginger. Reduce the mixer speed to low and add the milk mixture, mixing just until the dough barely comes together.

3 Turn the dough out onto a well-floured work surface and sprinkle about 2 tablespoons all-purpose flour on top of it. Knead the dough a few times, just until it doesn't stick to the work surface; do not overwork the dough. The inside of the dough should remain on the wet side. Gently roll out the dough into a ¾-inch-thick round.

4 Using a 2¼-inch fluted biscuit cutter, dipping the cutter into flour between cuts, cut out the scones (cut straight down and do not twist the cutter) and place 1½ inches apart on the prepared half-sheet pan. To get the

most scones out of the dough, cut out the scones close together in concentric circles from the outside in. Gather up the dough scraps, knead very lightly, roll out, and cut out more scones.

5 Beat the remaining egg and brush the tops of the scones lightly with it, being sure not to let the egg drip down the sides (which would inhibit a good rise).

6 Place the scones in the oven and immediately reduce the heat to 400°F. Bake until golden brown, 15 to 20 minutes. Cool on the pan for a few minutes and serve warm, or let cool completely.

Water Mill Biscuits

Makes 10 to 12 biscuits

One weekend when I was at our home in Water Mill, New York, I craved homemade biscuits. As luck would have it, the market was out of buttermilk. But I was not to be deterred. I could still make the biscuits by using a simple substitution: I stirred a small amount of lemon juice into whole milk and let it stand for about 20 minutes. Because buttermilk is nothing more than milk that has been soured by adding a culture (lactic acid bacteria), this technique yields a good alternative.

BAKER'S NOTE: To reheat baked biscuits, wrap them in aluminum foil and bake in a preheated 350°F oven for about 10 minutes.

¾ cup (168 grams) whole milk

1½ teaspoons fresh lemon juice

1¾ cups (249 grams) unbleached all-purpose flour, plus more as needed

1 tablespoon superfine sugar

2½ teaspoons baking powder

⅛ teaspoon fine sea salt

6 tablespoons (85 grams) unsalted butter, cut into ½-inch cubes and chilled

1 Position a rack in the center of the oven and preheat to 400°F. Line a half-sheet pan with parchment paper.

2 In a liquid measuring cup, combine the milk and lemon juice. Let stand in a warm place (for example, near the preheating oven) for about 20 minutes.

3 Sift the flour, sugar, baking powder, and salt into a medium bowl. Add the butter and toss to coat it with the flour mixture. Using a pastry blender, cut the butter into the flour, scraping off the blender as needed, until the mixture resembles coarse bread crumbs with some pea-sized pieces of butter. Using a wooden spoon, stir in the sour milk mixture and mix just until the dough clumps together.

4 Scrape the dough out onto a lightly floured surface and knead a few times, until it is smooth. Sprinkle the top of the dough with flour, and roll it out a little more than ¾ inch thick. Using a 2-inch fluted biscuit cutter, dipping the cutter into flour between cuts, cut out the biscuits (cut straight down and do not twist the cutter) and place 1 inch apart on the prepared half-sheet pan. To get the most biscuits out of the dough, cut out the biscuits close together in concentric circles from the outside in. Gently press the scraps together (do not overhandle the dough), and repeat rolling and cutting out until all of the dough is used.

5 Bake until the biscuits are well risen and golden brown, 15 to 20 minutes. Serve hot or warm.

Strawberry Shortcakes

Makes 8 servings

I love these shortcakes and have been serving them in our restaurants for more than twenty years. I learned to bake them from a wonderful baker and friend who was inspired by James Beard's recipe. Paired with vanilla-scented strawberries, they make for an easy spring or summer brunch. If you want to serve them as part of a bigger menu for a larger crowd, stamp out more cakes using a smaller biscuit cutter.

BAKER'S NOTE: To show off only the brilliant red color of strawberries, I avoid the white core. Instead, I hull the berries, then sit each one on a cutting board, hulled end down. Starting from the center of the top, I slice toward the edge at an angle, then rotate the berry 45 degrees and slice again, from the center outward. I continue rotating and slicing until all that's left is the pale center, which I discard.

Strawberries

2 pints (10 ¼ ounces; 290 grams) strawberries, washed, hulled, and sliced (see Baker's Note)

¼ cup (49 grams) superfine sugar

Seeds from ½ vanilla bean, preferably a Plumped Vanilla Bean (page 3), or ½ teaspoon pure vanilla extract

1½ cups (213 grams) unbleached all-purpose flour, plus more as needed

¼ cup (49 grams) superfine sugar

1½ teaspoons baking powder

¼ teaspoon fine sea salt

1½ teaspoons freshly grated orange zest

5 tablespoons (71 grams) unsalted butter, cut into ½-inch cubes and chilled, plus 1 tablespoon butter, softened

¾ cup (174 grams) heavy cream

2 tablespoons granulated sugar

Whipped Cream (page 50), for serving • Confectioners' sugar, for garnish

1 To prepare the strawberries: In a medium bowl, mix the strawberries with the superfine sugar and vanilla seeds. Let stand for at least 1 hour and no more than 3 hours before serving. This will allow the berries to release their juices and give you a nice fruit syrup.

2 Position a rack in the center of the oven and preheat to 375°F. Line a half-sheet pan with parchment paper.

3 Sift the flour, superfine sugar, baking powder, and salt into a medium bowl. Add the orange zest. Add the butter and toss to coat it with the flour mixture. Using a pastry blender, cut the butter into the flour, scraping off the blender as needed, until the mixture resembles coarse bread crumbs with some pea-sized pieces of butter. Using a wooden spoon, stir in the cream and mix just until the dough clumps together.

4 Scrape the dough out onto a lightly floured surface and knead a few times, until it is smooth. Sprinkle the top of the dough with flour and gently roll out to a ¾-inch-thick round. Using a 2¾-inch fluted biscuit cutter, dipping the cutter into flour between cuts, cut out shortcakes (cut straight down and do not twist the cutter) and place 1½ inches apart on the prepared half-sheet pan. To get the most shortcakes out of the dough, cut out the shortcakes close together in concentric circles from the outside in. Gather up the dough scraps and knead very lightly, roll out and cut out more cakes.

5 Brush the tops of the cakes with the softened butter and sprinkle with the granulated sugar. Bake until lightly browned, 18 to 20 minutes. Cool completely on the pan.

6 When ready to serve, split the shortcakes in half. Spoon the berries and their syrup onto the bottom halves, top with whipped cream, and cover with the tops. Lightly sift confectioners' sugar on top of each shortcake.

Jam Mandelbrot

Makes 2 dozen mandelbrot

Margaret Firestone was my earliest culinary mentor. Her specialty was the food of her native Hungary. It seems like yesterday that we enjoyed these biscotti-style cookies, called *mandelbrot* (Yiddish for "almond bread"), while chatting over a cup of coffee. Traditionally these are made with almonds, but Margaret used fruit preserves instead. She was always trying different store-bought preserves to fill her mandelbrot—I never knew what I was going to find inside. Being a jam maker has its advantages—I always have lots of fresh-from-the-pot spreads to choose from. But I have to confess I have my favorite flavors: strawberry, apricot, and orange. And I know Margaret would have loved those flavors as well.

4 cups (568 grams) unbleached all-purpose flour, plus more as needed

1 teaspoon baking powder

¼ teaspoon fine sea salt

12 tablespoons (171 grams) unsalted butter, cut into tablespoons, at cool room temperature

1 cup (196 grams) superfine sugar

2 large eggs, beaten

½ teaspoon pure vanilla extract

⅓ cup (75 grams) fresh orange juice

⅓ cup (103 grams) Strawberry Jam (page 178)

⅓ cup (103 grams) Apricot Spread (page 177) or Mandarin Orange Spread (page 176)

1 large egg white, beaten, for glazing

Turbinado sugar, for sprinkling

1 In a medium bowl, whisk the flour, baking powder, and salt. In the bowl of a heavy-duty mixer fitted with the paddle attachment, beat the butter on medium-high speed until smooth, about 1 minute. Gradually add the sugar and beat, occasionally scraping down the bowl with a silicone spatula, until light in color and texture, about 2 minutes. Gradually add the eggs and vanilla and beat, scraping the bowl occasionally, until well combined.

2 Reduce the mixer speed to low and add the flour mixture in two additions, alternating with the orange juice in one addition. Mix just until the dough clumps together and the sides of the bowl are almost clean.

3 Transfer the dough to a lightly floured work surface and knead a few times, until smooth. Divide the dough in half. Shape each portion into a 1-inch-thick rectangle, wrap in plastic wrap, and refrigerate until just firm, 15 to 20 minutes. (The dough can be refrigerated for up to 1 day, but it will be very hard; let it stand at room temperature for about 30 minutes before rolling out. The dough can also be frozen, double-wrapped in plastic, for up to 2 weeks. Defrost in the refrigerator overnight.)

4 Position the racks in the center and top third of the oven and preheat to 350°F. Line two half-sheet pans with parchment paper.

5 Remove the dough from the refrigerator. Lightly flour the work surface. Unwrap one piece of the dough and rap the edges on the work surface to help prevent cracking during rolling. Place the dough on the work surface, sprinkle the top with flour, and roll out into a 15 by 8½ by ¼-inch rectangle. Transfer the dough to a piece of parchment paper that is larger than the dough. Using a small offset spatula, spread the strawberry jam over the dough, leaving a 1-inch border around the edges. Fold the short ends over by 1 inch, then fold one long side over to cover the center third of the dough. Fold the remaining long side over the center to cover two-thirds of it. Use the parchment paper to carefully invert the dough seam side down onto one of the prepared half-sheet pans. Repeat with the second piece of dough, using the apricot spread, and place on the other prepared pan. Lightly brush the loaves with the beaten egg white. Sprinkle with the turbinado sugar.

6 Bake, switching the positions of the pans halfway through, until the loaves are golden brown, about 35 minutes. Cool on the pans for 10 minutes.

7 While the loaves are still warm, use the parchment paper to carefully slide the loaves, still on the paper, onto a cutting board. Using a serrated knife, cut each loaf at a slight angle into 1-inch-wide pieces. Set wire racks on the half-sheet pans. Using a wide offset spatula, transfer the mandelbrot to the racks, spacing them ½ inch apart.

8 Bake the mandelbrot until lightly toasted, 8 to 10 minutes. Cool completely on the racks on the pans. The mandelbrot can be stored in an airtight container at room temperature for up to 5 days.

TIPS FOR PERFECT CAKES

1 Choose the right size pan. For fluted tube pans, measure the pans by capacity rather than diameter to ensure that they can hold the batter. To measure a pan's volume, count how many cups of water are needed to fill the pan to the brim. For cake and loaf pans, select them based on their dimensions. Measure the length and width across the top, not the bottom.

2 Properly butter and flour the pan or pans by brushing the entire interior with very soft butter, using a soft-bristled pastry brush. Round brushes work better than flat ones, particularly for fluted pans. Be sure to get the butter into every crevice, then sprinkle the butter coating with a generous amount of flour, tilting the pan and shaking it to distribute the flour. Invert the pan and tap it to remove excess flour. If you see any uncoated or uneven spots, butter and flour them.

3 Take the time to cream the butter and sugar properly. It's crucial for getting the right volume and texture. For the best results, use a heavy-duty stand mixer fitted with a paddle attachment. You can use a handheld electric mixer, but increase the creaming time by 1 or 2 minutes. The butter and sugar must be beaten together at medium-high speed until the mixture is pale yellow. Stop the mixer and scrape down the sides of the bowl often.

4 Add the eggs slowly to prevent the batter from breaking or curdling. First beat the room-temperature eggs with a whisk. Then, with the mixer running, add them gradually to the creamed butter and sugar.

5 Carefully add the dry and wet ingredients. This final mixing step—alternately adding dry and wet ingredients on low speed—determines whether your cake will end up tender and evenly textured. Stop the machine occasionally and scrape the bottom and sides of the bowl to ensure a smooth batter. Once everything is added, scrape the bottom once again to incorporate every last bit.

6 When you think your cake is baked, check its doneness correctly. It's ready if the surface springs back when lightly pressed with your fingertip. But a more surefire technique is to insert a cake tester into the thickest part of the cake until the tip reaches the center, then pull the tester right back out, without jiggling it, and see if there are any crumbs on it. If not, it's done.

7 Let the cake cool in the pan (or pans) on a wire rack for 10 minutes before unmolding. In that time, the cake will pull away from the sides of the pan, making it easier to release it from the pan.

8 Unmold the cake carefully so that it stays beautifully intact: Center a wire rack on top of the pan. Holding the pan and the rack together, with oven mitts, flip both together and set down. The cake should come right out. If it doesn't, tap the pan against the rack. Then slowly lift the pan straight off the cake.

9 To keep a cake fresh if you're not eating it right away, wrap the cooled cake—not the cake plate—tightly in plastic wrap, with the wrap directly against the surface of the cake. Store at room temperature.

Lemon Yogurt Bundt Cake

Makes 10 to 12 servings

I pack this classic Bundt with lemon. I rub the zest into the sugar to release its fragrant oils and mix the juice with yogurt to accentuate its tang. What really gives the cake its bright burst, though, is the final soak in lemon syrup. This cake is beautiful as a Bundt, but the batter can also be baked in two 9 by 5 by 3-inch loaf pans.

Softened unsalted butter and flour, for the pan
3 cups (426 grams) unbleached all-purpose flour
½ teaspoon baking soda
¾ teaspoon fine sea salt
2 teaspoons freshly grated lemon zest (from 2 lemons)
2½ cups (490 grams) superfine sugar
⅔ cup (174 grams) plain yogurt
⅓ cup (75 grams) whole milk
3 tablespoons plus 1 teaspoon fresh lemon juice
1 cup (227 grams) unsalted butter, chilled and cut into ½-inch cubes
5 large eggs, at room temperature, beaten

Lemon Glaze

6 tablespoons (84 grams) fresh lemon juice • ½ cup (98 grams) superfine sugar

1 Position a rack in the center of the oven and preheat to 350°F. Butter and flour a 10-cup (9-inch) Bundt pan and tap out the excess flour.

2 Sift the flour, baking soda, and salt into a medium bowl. In another medium bowl, rub the lemon zest into the sugar with your fingertips. In a small bowl, whisk the yogurt, milk, and lemon juice.

3 In the bowl of a heavy-duty stand mixer fitted with the paddle attachment, beat the butter on high speed until smooth, about 1 minute. Gradually add the sugar mixture and continue beating, scraping the sides of the bowl often with a silicone spatula, until the mixture is very light in color and texture, about 5 minutes. Gradually beat in the eggs, scraping the sides of the bowl occasionally.

4 Reduce the mixer speed to low. Add the flour mixture in thirds, alternating with the yogurt mixture in two additions, scraping the sides of the bowl and beating briefly after each addition. Scrape the batter into the prepared pan. Smooth the top with the spatula.

5 Bake until the top of the cake springs back when gently pressed with your finger and a cake tester inserted into the center of the cake comes out clean, 45 minutes to 1 hour.

6 While the cake bakes, make the glaze: In a small bowl, stir the lemon juice and sugar until the sugar mostly dissolves. Let stand so that the sugar completely dissolves.

7 Cool the cake in the pan on a wire rack for 10 minutes. Invert the cake onto the rack, remove the cake pan, and set the rack over a half-sheet pan. Use a round pastry brush to gently brush the glaze all over the cake, letting each addition soak in before adding the next; be sure to brush the parts around the center hole. Cool completely. The cake can be stored, wrapped in plastic wrap, at room temperature for up to 3 days.

New York Crumb Cake

Makes 10 to 12 servings

Sometimes it's the simplest things that are the hardest to perfect. In this case, I wanted just the right proportion of buttery spiced crumbs to tender golden cake. It turns out using a 9-inch square cake pan is key. An 8-inch pan gave me too tall a cake, a 10-inch one, a too-flat cake. Now everything about this classic cake is just right.

Softened unsalted butter and flour, for the pan

Crumb Topping

1½ cups (213 grams) unbleached all-purpose flour
⅓ cup (65 grams) superfine sugar
⅓ cup (65 grams) packed light brown sugar
½ teaspoon ground cinnamon
¼ teaspoon fine sea salt
8 tablespoons (114 grams) unsalted butter, melted and cooled
1 teaspoon pure vanilla extract

2 cups (284 grams) unbleached all-purpose flour
1½ teaspoons baking powder
¼ teaspoon fine sea salt
1 teaspoon pure vanilla extract
1⅓ cups (261 grams) superfine sugar
⅔ cup (152 grams) unsalted butter, cut into ½-inch cubes, at room temperature
2 large eggs, at room temperature, beaten
1 cup (242 grams) sour cream

1 Position a rack in the center of the oven and preheat to 350°F. Butter and flour a 9 by 9 by 2-inch cake pan and tap out the excess flour.

2 To make the crumb topping: In a medium bowl, whisk the flour, superfine sugar, brown sugar, cinnamon, and salt. Add the butter and vanilla and mix with your fingers until combined and crumbly. Set aside.

3 Sift the flour, baking powder, and salt into a medium bowl. In a small bowl, rub the vanilla into the sugar. In the bowl of a heavy-duty stand mixer fitted with the paddle attachment, beat the butter on high speed until smooth, about 1 minute. Gradually add the sugar mixture and continue beating, scraping the sides of the bowl often with a silicone spatula, until the mixture is very light in color and texture, about 5 minutes. Gradually beat in the eggs, scraping the sides of the bowl occasionally.

4 Reduce the mixer speed to low. Add the flour mixture in thirds, alternating with two additions of the sour cream, scraping the sides of the bowl and beating briefly after each addition. Scrape the batter into the prepared pan. Smooth the top with the spatula. Squeeze handfuls of the crumb topping, then break into small clumps and sprinkle the entire surface of the batter with the clumps and crumbs.

5 Bake until the crumbs are golden brown and a cake tester inserted into the center of the cake comes out clean, about 55 minutes.

6 Cool completely in the pan on a wire rack before serving. The cake can be stored in the pan, wrapped in plastic wrap, at room temperature for up to 2 days.

Apple Custard Cake

Makes 8 to 10 servings

Hidden among my stacks of cookbooks was an old spiral-bound Jewish community cookbook. What a treasure. Its typewritten pages contained family recipes from generations of cooks. I was especially intrigued by a cake that called for baking a layer of apples in custard over a butter cake batter. I've adapted the original to create a unique, irresistible breakfast cake. The top layer of thin apple slices set in a classic custard fuses into the sturdy yet tender cake. I like to bake this in a special Italian cake pan, which has a large tube in the center. It lets the batter stay moist as it sets; a pan without a center tube will overcook the edges before the middle bakes through. My pan is 9 inches in diameter and 2½ inches high, with a 2½-inch center tube. I doubt you'll be able to find the same pan, though—I'm not even sure where I got mine. Use a shallow 8- or 9-inch tube pan instead.

Softened unsalted butter and flour, for the pan

1½ cups (213 grams) unbleached all-purpose flour

1½ teaspoons baking powder

⅛ teaspoon fine sea salt

1 teaspoon pure vanilla extract

¾ cup (147 grams) superfine sugar

½ cup (112 grams) whole milk

2 tablespoons heavy cream

4 tablespoons (57 grams) unsalted butter, chilled and cut into ½-inch cubes

1 large egg, at room temperature, beaten

1 large Honeycrisp apple (8 ounces; 227 grams), peeled, cored, and cut into ¼-inch slices

Custard

1 large egg yolk

2 tablespoons heavy cream

1 tablespoon superfine sugar

½ teaspoon pure vanilla extract

White sanding or turbinado sugar, for sprinkling

1 Position a rack in the center of the oven and preheat to 350°F. Butter and flour a 9-inch shallow tube pan and tap out the excess flour.

2 Sift the flour, baking powder, and salt into a medium bowl. In a small bowl, rub the vanilla into the superfine sugar. In another small bowl, mix the milk and cream. In the bowl of a heavy-duty stand mixer fitted with the paddle attachment, beat the butter on high speed until smooth, about 1 minute. Gradually add the sugar mixture and continue beating, scraping the sides of the bowl often with a silicone spatula, until the mixture is very light in color and texture, about 3 minutes. Gradually beat in the egg, scraping the sides of the bowl occasionally.

3 Reduce the mixer speed to low. Add the flour mixture in thirds, alternating with two additions of the milk mixture, scraping the sides of the bowl and beating briefly after each addition. Scrape the batter into the prepared pan. Smooth the top with the spatula. Press the apple slices into the cake batter, overlapping them slightly.

4 To make the custard: In a small bowl, whisk the egg yolk, cream, superfine sugar, and vanilla. Pour the custard mixture on top and tilt the pan to distribute the custard evenly. Sprinkle with sanding sugar on top.

5 Bake until the top is golden brown and a cake tester inserted into the cake comes out clean, about 25 minutes.

6 Cool completely in the pan on a wire rack. Run a small offset spatula around the edges of the cake and the center tube to release the cake. Place a flat, rimless 10-inch plate on top of the cake, quickly and carefully flip the pan and plate together, and lift off the pan. Place a flat serving plate over the cake and immediately flip both plates, then lift off the top plate. Serve immediately, or cover tightly with plastic wrap and refrigerate for up to 3 days.

Marble Cake

Makes 10 to 12 servings

Chocolate for breakfast feels a bit too indulgent—unless it comes in the form of the dark swirls in this cake. The blend of cocoa powder and espresso is neither overly sweet nor excessively rich. It adds a deep flavor to this fine-crumbed almond-scented cake.

Softened unsalted butter and flour, for the pan

2 cups (284 grams) unbleached all-purpose flour

2 teaspoons baking powder

½ teaspoon fine sea salt

1 teaspoon pure vanilla extract

½ teaspoon pure almond extract

1½ cups (294 grams) plus 3 tablespoons superfine sugar

12 tablespoons (171 grams) unsalted butter, cut into ½-inch cubes, at room temperature

4 large eggs, at room temperature, beaten

⅓ cup (43 grams) Dutch-processed cocoa powder

⅓ cup (75 grams) brewed espresso, cooled

1 Position a rack in the center of the oven and preheat to 350°F. Butter and flour a 10-cup (9-inch) Bundt pan and tap out the excess flour.

2 Sift the flour, baking powder, and salt into a medium bowl. In another medium bowl, rub the vanilla and almond extracts into 1½ cups sugar. In the bowl of a heavy-duty stand mixer fitted with the paddle attachment, beat the butter on high speed until smooth, about 1 minute. Gradually add the sugar mixture and continue beating, scraping the sides of the bowl often with a silicone spatula, until the mixture is very light in color and texture, about 5 minutes. Gradually beat in the eggs, scraping the sides of the bowl occasionally.

3 Reduce the mixer speed to low and gradually add the flour mixture, beating until just combined. Scrape the bowl, then beat on medium-high speed for 10 seconds, to ensure everything is well mixed.

4 In a medium bowl, whisk the cocoa, espresso, and remaining 3 tablespoons sugar to dissolve the cocoa. Transfer 1½ cups batter to the cocoa mixture and fold in with a silicone spatula until smooth. Using a 2½-inch-diameter ice-cream scoop, alternate scoops of the vanilla and chocolate batters into the prepared pan. With a chopstick, swirl the batters together to marbleize them, taking care not to touch the sides of the pan. Gently smooth the top.

5 Bake until the top of the cake springs back when gently pressed with your finger and a cake tester inserted into the center of the cake comes out clean, about 45 minutes.

6 Cool in the pan on a wire rack for 10 minutes. Invert the cake onto the rack to cool completely. The cake can be stored, wrapped in plastic wrap, at room temperature for up to 3 days.

Breads and Yeasted Treats

YEAST IS INCOMPARABLE IN ITS ABILITY TO CREATE FLAVORFUL BREAKFAST STAPLES, FROM LOVELY LOAVES OF BREAD TO SWEET, BUTTERY pastries. It's hard to believe I briefly considered not including bread recipes in this book. It seemed troublesome to wake up early enough to bake a freshly risen loaf for breakfast. At our bakery, my crew works through the night to achieve that. But then I realized that homemade breads for the morning meal don't necessarily have to come out of the oven as the sun rises. Loaves made the afternoon or night before are ideal for French toast, and also can't be beat as regular toast. Not only do they taste so much better than store-bought bread, they also fill the house with warm, mouthwatering scents.

What should be served hot out of the oven are my tender yeasted treats. All five of these delicious recipes are made from the same basic dough. Enriched with butter and sour cream, it develops a golden crust and soft crumb as it bakes. Lightly sweetened, it works well with both sweet and salty additions. Best of all, the dough can be prepared ahead and baked from the refrigerator, so you can sleep in a little and still bake beautiful yeasted pastries.

KEY INGREDIENT

Yeast: Fresh yeast, also known as compressed or cake yeast, is what I use. It results in a better rise than dry yeast and doesn't need to be dissolved in warm water before using. It's often sold in 2-ounce or ⅔-ounce foil-wrapped cakes in the refrigerated section of the supermarket. It spoils easily, so keep it in the refrigerator, tightly wrapped in plastic wrap, and use it up quickly. But active dry yeast, readily available in all supermarkets, works well in these recipes too. It can be kept for a longer period of time in a cool, dry place. If you don't plan to use it regularly, buy the yeast in a strip of three ¼-ounce envelopes. Avid bakers can purchase a whole jar. Active dry yeast must be dissolved in warm water before use. If the water is too hot, though, it can kill the yeast. If you're not sure about the water temperature, use a thermometer to see if the water is between 105° and 115°F, the ideal range for dissolving the yeast.

TOOL KIT

Loaf Pans: The two sizes of loaf pans that I use are 8 by 4 by 2½ inches and 9 by 5 by 3 inches. While they may look similar, there is a 2-cup volume difference between them. Don't substitute one for the other, or you'll end up with a sadly shallow loaf or one that spills out of the pan. Avoid pans with dark surfaces, which brown the crust too much, and glass or ceramic pans, which don't brown the crust enough. Heavy aluminum pans with a dull finish are just right.

Tall Kitchen Plastic Bags: You probably already stock these garbage bags at home. If not, pick up a box—make sure you buy unscented bags. They're used in these recipes to create a humid chamber for proofing dough.

TIPS FOR PERFECT BREAD

1 Make sure the yeast is alive. Buy it fresh, well before its best-by date, and use it shortly after purchasing. If you're not sure whether or not it's still alive, check to make sure it bubbles: Mix fresh yeast with a little sugar or dissolve active dry yeast in a little warm—not hot—water.

2 Start by adding only half of the flour. Baking bread is as much an art as it is a science. Changes in temperature and humidity will alter the amount of flour you need for the dough. Then add only enough of the remaining flour to form a rough dough that leaves the sides of the bowl. If necessary, you can always knead in a bit more flour by hand if the dough is still too sticky after kneading.

3 Don't let the dough dry out during its first rise. Place the kneaded dough ball in a buttered bowl and turn to coat it with the butter, then cover the bowl tightly with plastic wrap.

4 Choose a warm, draft-free spot for the dough to rise and double its original volume. Make sure the chosen area is not too warm, though. If it is, the dough can overferment and end up misshapen and too yeasty in taste. If the dough looks doubled, you can double-check its readiness by gently pressing a fingertip ½ inch into the dough. If it leaves an impression, it's ready.

5 To build the perfect proofing box, all you need is a pan, a tall glass of hot water, and a tall kitchen plastic bag. Slide the pan with the shaped loaves into the bag, place the glass in the center of the pan, and wave the bag to fill it with air. Immediately seal the bag, using one of the ties that came with the bags. The glass ensures that the bag won't touch the dough and mar the tops and the water adds warm humidity to the "box."

6 Double-check the bread's doneness. You can see when the crust has become a gorgeous golden brown, of course, but you want to make sure the dough isn't still raw inside. The best test is to quickly flip the bread out of the pan and tap the bottom: it should sound hollow, not dense.

7 Cool the loaves in the pans for 5 minutes only. They need that time to set, but they should be unmolded once that time is up, or they will steam and their crusts will soften.

Great Bread

Makes 2 loaves

This may be "white bread," but it's full of mildly sweet grain flavor. It's tender but not at all flabby, with a thin, delicate crust. I'm grateful to my friend and colleague Susan Rosenfeld for sharing this treasure many years ago. We originally made it at the bakery as a rendition of the old New England classic, anadama bread. The recipe starts with a cornmeal–crème fraîche mixture that brings both heartiness and tenderness to the crumb and complex yet subtle tangy notes. This loaf easily transitions from breakfast toast or French toast to lunchtime sandwiches.

1 cup (160 grams) very finely ground yellow cornmeal, plus more for sprinkling

2 teaspoons fine sea salt

¼ cup (49 grams) plus 2 tablespoons superfine sugar

2¼ cups (504 grams) boiling water

¼ cup (71 grams) crème fraîche or sour cream

2 tablespoons (28 grams) crumbled compressed yeast or 3½ teaspoons (11 grams) active dry yeast

3½ cups (508 grams) bread flour

1½ cups (213 grams) unbleached all-purpose flour, plus more as needed

Softened unsalted butter, for the bowl and pans

Melted butter, for glazing the loaves

1 In the bowl of a heavy-duty stand mixer, whisk the cornmeal, salt, and ¼ cup sugar. Whisk in the boiling water until the mixture is smooth. (If using dry yeast, whisk in 2 cups of the boiling water.) Whisk in the crème fraîche. Let stand until completely cooled.

2 If using compressed yeast, in a small bowl, combine the crumbled yeast and the remaining 2 tablespoons sugar. Let stand until the yeast gives off some moisture, about 3 minutes, then whisk well to dissolve the yeast. Whisk into the cooled cornmeal mixture. (Or, if using active dry yeast, in a small bowl, sprinkle the yeast over ¼ cup lukewarm, 105° to 115°F, water. Let stand until the yeast softens, about 5 minutes, then stir to dissolve. Whisk into the cooled cornmeal mixture, along with the remaining 2 tablespoons sugar.) Attach the bowl to the mixer and fit the mixer with the paddle attachment.

3 In a medium bowl, whisk the bread and all-purpose flours. On low speed, gradually add enough of the flour to the yeast mixture to form a soft, rough dough that cleans the sides of the bowl. Replace the paddle attachment with the dough hook. Knead on medium-low speed, adding more flour if needed, until the dough is smooth, soft, and elastic, about 8 minutes.

4 Transfer the dough to a lightly floured work surface. Knead briefly to check the dough's texture: It should feel slightly sticky but not stick to the work surface. Knead in more flour only if needed. Butter a large bowl.

Shape the dough into a taut ball. Place in the bowl, turn to coat with butter, and turn smooth side up. Cover tightly with plastic wrap. Let stand in a warm place until the dough doubles in volume, 1 to 1½ hours.

5 Turn the dough out onto a lightly floured work surface. Cut it in half and shape each piece into a ball. Cover with plastic wrap and let stand for 15 minutes.

6 Butter two 8 by 4 by 2½-inch loaf pans. Gently press one ball of dough to deflate it. Pat the dough gently into an 8-inch-long rectangle. Starting from a long side, roll up and shape into an 8-inch-long loaf, then pinch the seam closed. Place seam side down in one of the prepared pans. Repeat with the remaining dough. Place the pans on a half-sheet pan.

7 Choose a warm spot in the kitchen for proofing. Slip the pan with the loaf pans into a tall kitchen plastic bag. Place a tall glass of hot water on the pan between the loaves to keep the bag from touching the dough. Wave the bag to inflate it and then tightly close it, trapping air in the bag. Let stand until the loaves gently dome about an inch above the tops of the pans, about 45 minutes.

8 Position a rack in the center of the oven and preheat to 350°F.

9 Remove the glass from the bag, then remove the pan with the loaf pans. Brush the tops of the loaves lightly all over with melted butter. Using a single-edge razor or sharp serrated knife, cut a shallow (¼-inch-deep) slash down the center of each loaf. Lightly sprinkle with cornmeal. Bake the loaves on the half-sheet pan until they are browned and the bottoms sound hollow when tapped, 35 to 40 minutes.

10 Cool in the pans on a wire rack for 5 minutes. Remove the loaves from the pans and cool on the rack.

Sarabeth's House Bread

Makes 2 loaves

This bread has graced the display case ever since we opened our first bakery. It has an irresistible nutty-sweet flavor and grainy texture—it also slices beautifully. That's why I give you this recipe once again (it made its debut in my first cookbook). At the restaurants, we use it for our club sandwiches and serve it sliced and toasted for breakfast and brunch. At home, I rely on it for morning toast and French toast as well.

2 tablespoons (28 grams) crumbled compressed yeast or 3½ teaspoons (11 grams) active dry yeast

¼ cup (85 grams) honey

2¼ cups (504 grams) cold water

2¾ cups (413 grams) stone-ground whole wheat flour

2¾ cups (399 grams) bread flour

2 tablespoons very finely ground yellow cornmeal

2 tablespoons poppy seeds

2 tablespoons sesame seeds

1½ teaspoons fine sea salt

2 tablespoons raw hulled sunflower seeds

Softened unsalted butter, for the bowl and pans

1 large egg, beaten, for the glaze

1 If using compressed yeast, in the bowl of a heavy-duty stand mixer, combine the crumbled yeast and honey. Let stand until the yeast gives off some moisture, about 3 minutes, then whisk well to dissolve the yeast. Add the water and whisk well to combine. (Or, if using active dry yeast, in a small bowl, sprinkle the yeast over ¼ cup lukewarm, 105° to 115°F, water. Let stand until the yeast softens, about 5 minutes, then stir to dissolve. Pour into the mixer bowl. Add 2 cups cold water and the honey and whisk to combine.) Attach the bowl to the mixer and fit the mixer with the paddle attachment.

2 In a large bowl, combine the whole wheat flour, 2¼ cups bread flour, the cornmeal, poppy seeds, sesame seeds, and salt. On low speed, gradually add the flour mixture to the yeast mixture and beat until a dough begins to form. Gradually add enough of the remaining ½ cup bread flour to form a rough dough that cleans the sides of the bowl. Replace the paddle attachment with the dough hook. Knead on medium-low speed, adding more flour only if needed, until the dough is smooth and slightly sticky, about 5 minutes; the dough should be soft. During the last minute or so, add the sunflower seeds.

3 Transfer the dough to a clean, unfloured work surface. Knead briefly to check the dough's texture: It should feel slightly sticky but not stick to the work surface. Knead in more flour only if needed. Butter a large bowl. Shape the dough into a taut ball. Place in the bowl, turn to coat with butter, and turn smooth side up. Cover tightly with plastic wrap. Let stand in a warm place until the dough doubles in volume, 1 to 1½ hours.

4 Turn the dough out onto a lightly floured work surface. Cut it in half and shape each piece into a ball. Cover with plastic wrap and let stand for 15 minutes.

5 Butter two 8 by 4 by 2½-inch loaf pans. Gently press one ball of dough to deflate it. Pat the dough gently into an 8-inch-long rectangle. Starting from a long side, roll up and shape into an 8-inch-long loaf, then pinch the seam closed. Place seam side down in one of the prepared pans. Repeat with the remaining dough. Place the pans on a half-sheet pan.

6 Choose a warm spot in the kitchen for proofing. Slip the pan with the loaf pans into a tall kitchen plastic bag. Place a tall glass of hot water on the pan between the loaves to keep the bag from touching the dough. Wave the bag to inflate it and then tightly close it, trapping air in the bag. Let stand until the loaves gently dome about an inch above the tops of the pans, about 45 minutes.

7 Position a rack in the center of the oven and preheat to 375°F.

8 Remove the glass from the bag, then remove the pan with the loaf pans. Brush the tops of the loaves lightly all over with the beaten egg. Bake the loaves on the half-sheet pan until they are browned and the bottoms sound hollow when tapped, 35 to 40 minutes.

9 Cool in the pans on a wire rack for 5 minutes. Remove the loaves from the pans and cool completely on the rack.

Apple-Cinnamon Bread

Makes 2 loaves

On the weekends, all of our restaurants use this bread for our signature Apple-Cinnamon French Toast (page 93) at brunch. I sometimes wonder if that's why the crowds wait for a table. The thin apple slices break up when mixed into the dough, adding extra moisture to the soft spiced loaf. On its own, it's a welcome taste of fall. Toasted and slathered with ricotta and drizzled with honey, it's simply heaven.

1 tablespoon plus 2 teaspoons (22 grams) crumbled compressed yeast or 1 tablespoon (9 grams) active dry yeast

5 tablespoons (60 grams) superfine sugar

¼ cup (56 grams) cold whole milk

⅔ cup (149 grams) cold water

1 large egg yolk

1 teaspoon pure vanilla extract

2 large Granny Smith apples (1½ pounds; 680 grams), peeled, cored, and cut into ¼-inch slices

¼ teaspoon ground cinnamon

4 cups (568 grams) unbleached all-purpose flour, plus more as needed

1¼ teaspoons fine sea salt

4 tablespoons (57 grams) unsalted butter, cut into tablespoons, at room temperature

Softened unsalted butter, for the bowl and pans

1 If using compressed yeast, in the bowl of a heavy-duty stand mixer, combine the crumbled yeast and 3 tablespoons sugar. Let stand until the yeast gives off some moisture, about 3 minutes, then whisk well to dissolve the yeast. Add the milk, water, egg yolk, and vanilla and whisk well to combine. (Or, if using active dry yeast, in a small bowl, sprinkle the yeast over ⅓ cup lukewarm, 105° to 115°F, water. Let stand until the yeast softens, about 5 minutes, then stir to dissolve. Pour into the mixer bowl. Add the milk, egg yolk, vanilla, ⅓ cup cold water, and 3 tablespoons sugar and whisk to combine.)

2 In a medium bowl, toss the apple slices with the cinnamon and the remaining 2 tablespoons sugar until coated.

3 Attach the bowl to the mixer and fit the mixer with the paddle attachment. On low speed, gradually add 2 cups flour to the yeast mixture, then add the salt. Add the butter 1 tablespoon at a time, waiting for each addition to be incorporated before adding the next. Add the apple mixture and continue beating until the apples break up, about 5 minutes. Gradually add only enough of the remaining 2 cups flour to form a rough dough. Replace the paddle attachment with the dough hook. Knead on medium-low speed, adding more flour only if needed, until the dough cleans the sides of the bowl, about 5 minutes.

4 Transfer the dough to a clean work surface. Knead briefly to check the dough's texture: It should feel slightly sticky but not stick to the work surface. Knead in more flour only if needed. Butter a large bowl. Shape the

dough into a taut ball. Place in the bowl, turn to coat with butter, and turn smooth side up. Cover tightly with plastic wrap. Let stand in a warm place until the dough doubles in volume, 1 to 1½ hours.

5 Turn the dough out onto a lightly floured work surface. Cut it in half and shape each piece into a ball. Cover with plastic wrap and let stand for 15 minutes.

6 Butter two 8 by 4 by 2½-inch loaf pans. Line the bottoms of the pans with parchment paper and butter the parchment. Gently press one ball of dough to deflate it. Pat the dough gently into an 8-inch-long rectangle. Starting from a long side, roll up and shape into an 8-inch-long loaf, then pinch the seam closed. Place seam side down in one of the prepared pans. Repeat with the remaining dough. Place the pans on a half-sheet pan.

7 Choose a warm spot in the kitchen for proofing. Slip the pan with the loaf pans into a tall kitchen plastic bag. Place a tall glass of hot water on the pan between the loaves to keep the bag from touching the dough. Wave the bag to inflate it and then tightly close it, trapping air in the bag. Let stand until the loaves gently dome about an inch above the tops of the pans, about 45 minutes.

8 Position a rack in the center of the oven and preheat to 350°F.

9 Remove the glass from the bag, then remove the pan with the loaf pans. Bake the loaves on the half-sheet pan for 35 minutes. Cover the loaves loosely with aluminum foil and continue baking until the tops are golden brown and an instant-read thermometer inserted into the center of the loaves reads 210°F, about 25 minutes longer.

10 Cool in the pans on a wire rack for 5 minutes. Remove the loaves from the pans, remove the parchment paper, and cool completely on the rack.

Challah Loaves

Makes 2 loaves

There would be no Fat-and-Fluffy French Toast (page 91) at our restaurants without this classic Jewish bread. Golden with eggs, challah is traditionally eaten at the Sabbath meal. It's often braided into a twist, but it tastes just as good when simply baked in two loaf pans. The pans help the dough hold its shape when baking, which makes for very uniform slices that are ideal for French toast.

2 tablespoons (28 grams) crumbled compressed yeast or 3½ teaspoons (11 grams) active dry yeast

¼ cup (85 grams) honey

1 cup (224 grams) cold water

¼ cup (55 grams) corn oil, preferably cold-pressed, or other vegetable oil

3 large eggs

2 large egg yolks

4½ cups (639 grams) unbleached all-purpose flour, plus more as needed

1½ teaspoons fine sea salt

Corn oil or vegetable oil, for the bowl and pans

1 If using compressed yeast, in the bowl of a heavy-duty stand mixer, combine the crumbled yeast and honey. Let stand until the yeast gives off some moisture, about 3 minutes, then whisk well to dissolve the yeast. Add the water, oil, 2 eggs, and 2 egg yolks and whisk well to combine. (Or, if using active dry yeast, in a small bowl, sprinkle the yeast over ¼ cup lukewarm, 105° to 115°F, water. Let stand until the yeast softens, about 5 minutes, then stir to dissolve. Pour into the mixer bowl. Add the honey, ¾ cup cold water, oil, 2 eggs, and 2 egg yolks and whisk to combine.) Attach the bowl to the mixer and fit the mixer with the paddle attachment.

2 On low speed, gradually add half of the flour to the yeast mixture, and then add the salt. Gradually add enough of the remaining flour to form a soft, rough dough that cleans the sides of the bowl. Replace the paddle attachment with the dough hook. Knead on medium-low speed, adding more flour only if needed, until the dough is smooth, soft, and elastic, about 6 minutes.

3 Transfer the dough to a lightly floured work surface. Knead briefly to check the dough's texture: It should feel slightly sticky but not stick to the work surface. Knead in more flour only if needed. Lightly oil a large bowl. Shape the dough into a taut ball. Place in the bowl, turn to coat with oil, and turn smooth side up. Cover tightly with plastic wrap. Let stand in a warm place until the dough doubles in volume, about 1½ hours.

4 Working carefully to preserve the dough's light and puffy texture, turn the dough out onto a clean, unfloured work surface. (Do not knead the dough.) Cut the dough in half and shape each piece into a ball. Cover with plastic wrap and let stand for 15 minutes.

5 Oil two 8 by 4 by 2½-inch loaf pans. Gently press one ball of dough to deflate it. Pat the dough gently into an 8-inch-long rectangle. Starting from a long side, roll up and shape into an 8-inch-long loaf, then pinch the seam closed. Place seam side down in one of the prepared pans. Repeat with the remaining dough. Place the pans on a half-sheet pan.

6 Choose a warm spot in the kitchen for proofing. Slip the pan with the loaf pans into a tall kitchen plastic bag. Place a tall glass of hot water on the pan between the loaves to keep the bag from touching the dough. Wave the bag to inflate it and then tightly close it, trapping air in the bag. Let stand until the loaves gently dome about an inch above the tops of the pans, 45 to 60 minutes.

7 Position a rack in the center of the oven and preheat to 375°F.

8 Remove the glass from the bag, then remove the pan with the loaf pans. Beat the remaining egg. Brush the tops of the loaves lightly all over with the beaten egg. Bake the loaves on the half-sheet pan for 15 minutes. Reduce the oven temperature to 350°F and continue baking until the loaves are golden brown and the bottoms sound hollow when tapped, 30 to 40 minutes longer. If the loaves seem to be browning too deeply, cover them loosely with aluminum foil.

9 Cool in the pans on a wire rack for 5 minutes. Remove the loaves from the pans and cool completely on the rack.

Whole Wheat English Muffins

Makes 10 muffins

I couldn't imagine my tried-and-true English muffins being any tastier, but then I swapped in some whole wheat flour for part of the all-purpose and coated the rings with wheat bran. Wow! The deeper wheat flavor added layers of complexity without compromising the muffin's versatility. I bake English muffins in metal entremet rings, which turn the dough into tall mushroom shapes. It's worth the effort to get these rings, which are available at specialty cookware stores. The shape is not only stunning, it also gives you the ideal texture.

BAKER'S NOTE: The batter must be chilled for at least 4 hours, but no longer than 8 hours, for the best results and flavor. You can make the dough in the morning and bake the muffins later in the day after chilling or make them a day ahead.

1 cup (224 grams) whole milk

1 cup (224 grams) water

2½ tablespoons unsalted butter, cut into small pieces

2 tablespoons superfine sugar

1 teaspoon fine sea salt

2 tablespoons (28 grams) crumbled compressed yeast or 3½ teaspoons (11 grams) active dry yeast

1 large egg, beaten

2¾ cups (391 grams) unbleached all-purpose flour

1 cup plus 3 tablespoons (178 grams) stone-ground whole wheat flour

Softened unsalted butter, for the rings

½ cup (30 grams) wheat bran, for the rings

1 At least 4 hours, and up to 8 hours, before making the muffins, prepare the batter: In a medium saucepan, bring the milk, water (if using dry yeast, use ¾ cup water), butter, sugar, and salt to a simmer over medium heat, stirring often to dissolve the butter. Transfer to the bowl of a heavy-duty stand mixer and cool to room temperature.

2 Sprinkle the compressed yeast into the mixer bowl and let stand for 5 minutes, then stir to dissolve. (Or, if using dry yeast, in a small bowl, sprinkle the yeast over ¼ cup lukewarm, 105° to 115°F, water. Let stand until the yeast softens, about 5 minutes, then stir to dissolve. Pour into the mixer bowl.) Stir the egg into the yeast mixture. Attach the bowl to the mixer and fit the mixer with the paddle attachment.

3 In a medium bowl, combine the all-purpose and whole wheat flours. On low speed, gradually beat the flour mixture into the yeast mixture to make a sticky batter. Increase the speed to high and beat for 30 seconds. Remove the bowl from the mixer and scrape down the sides of the bowl with a silicone spatula. Cover the bowl tightly with plastic wrap and refrigerate for at least 4 hours, or up to 8 hours.

4 Butter the insides of 12 metal entremet rings (3 inches in diameter and 1½ inches tall). Place the bran in a small bowl and coat the insides of the rings with some of it. Reserve the remaining bran. Line a half-sheet pan with parchment paper. Arrange the rings on the parchment, spacing them about 1½ inches apart. Sprinkle a light, even coating of bran into each ring (approximately ¼ teaspoon per ring).

5 Stir down the chilled batter; it will be very sticky. Using a 2½-inch-diameter ice-cream scoop dipped in cold water, scoop a level portion of dough into each ring. Lightly sprinkle the tops with the remaining bran.

6 Choose a warm spot in the kitchen for proofing. Slip the pan with the rings into a tall kitchen plastic bag. Place two tall glasses of hot water on the pan between the rings to keep the bag from touching the batter. Wave the bag to inflate it and tightly close it, trapping air in the bag. Make sure the plastic does not touch the batter. Let stand until the batter just begins to dome over the tops of the rings, about 1½ hours.

7 Position a rack in the bottom third of the oven and preheat to 350°F.

8 Carefully remove the glasses from the bag, then remove the pan with the rings. Bake the English muffins until the tops are golden brown, about 25 minutes. Let stand for 5 minutes, then remove the muffins from the rings, protecting your hands with a kitchen towel. (If the baked muffins are left in the rings too long, the muffins will steam and get a "cinched waist" look.) Cool slightly and serve warm, or cool to room temperature, split crosswise into thirds or quarters, and lightly toast before serving.

Spiced Whole Wheat English Muffins with Raisins: Add 1½ teaspoons ground cinnamon to the flour mixture. After the batter has come together in the mixer, add 1 cup (160 grams) raisins.

Popovers

Makes 1 dozen popovers

Popovers are pure magic. Although we've been serving them at our restaurants for ages, I still marvel every time they come out of the pan. Just beneath the crisp shell is a wonderfully moist eggy layer, and then a pocket that is ideal for stuffing. I'm happy to eat popovers plain or filled simply with a spread for a light breakfast, but I also enjoy stuffing them with scrambled eggs (page 195) for a more substantial meal.

SPECIAL EQUIPMENT: Popover pans really work best here. I tested this batter in muffin tins as well, but the popovers didn't rise and hollow out as dramatically. The result neither looked as impressive nor tasted as good.

Softened unsalted butter, for the pans
5 large eggs, at room temperature
2 cups (448 grams) whole milk
¼ teaspoon fine sea salt
2 tablespoons unsalted butter, melted and cooled
1½ cups (213 grams) unbleached all-purpose flour

1 Position a rack in the center of the oven and preheat to 400°F. Brush the insides and rims of 12 nonstick popover cups with softened butter.

2 In a large deep bowl, combine the eggs, milk, and salt and blend with an immersion (stick) blender until smooth. While blending, drizzle in the melted butter, then gradually add the flour and continue blending until very smooth. (Alternatively, in a stand blender, combine the eggs, milk, and salt and puree until smooth. With the machine running, drizzle in the melted butter. Add the flour and blend until very smooth.) Strain the mixture through a fine-mesh sieve into a measuring cup with a spout.

3 Place the prepared pans in the oven and heat for 2 minutes.

4 Carefully divide the batter among the popover cups. Return the pans to the oven and bake for 20 minutes. Reduce the oven temperature to 350°F and continue baking until the popovers are golden brown and crowning above the pan, about 10 minutes.

5 Carefully remove the popovers from the pan and transfer to a wire rack. Serve hot or warm.

Yeasted Sour Cream Dough

Makes two 1½-pound pieces of dough

There's nothing this dough can't do. Buttery and tender, it's the versatile foundation of the following five recipes. It has all the richness of a croissant dough without the labor-intensive rolling. And the generous amount of sour cream in the dough gives it a more complex taste. The baked dough tastes like equal parts pastry, bread, and cake, making it the ultimate morning treat. It's easy to make and can be kept handy in the freezer.

2½ tablespoons (35 grams) crumbled compressed yeast or 4¼ teaspoons (14 grams) active dry yeast

⅓ cup (65 grams) superfine sugar

⅔ cup (161 grams) sour cream

½ teaspoon fresh lemon juice

¼ teaspoon pure vanilla extract

2 large egg yolks

¾ cup (168 grams) whole milk

4½ cups (639 grams) unbleached all-purpose flour, plus more as needed

½ teaspoon fine sea salt

15 tablespoons (212 grams) unsalted butter, cut into tablespoons, well softened

Softened unsalted butter, for the bowl

1 If using compressed yeast, in the bowl of a heavy-duty stand mixer, combine the crumbled yeast and sugar. Let stand until the yeast gives off some moisture, about 3 minutes, then whisk well to dissolve the yeast. Add the sour cream, lemon juice, vanilla, and egg yolks and whisk well to combine. Whisk in the milk until smooth. (Or, if using active dry yeast, in a small bowl, sprinkle the yeast over ¼ cup lukewarm, 105° to 115°F, milk. Let stand until the yeast softens, about 5 minutes, then stir to dissolve. Pour into the mixer bowl. Add the sour cream, lemon juice, vanilla, and egg yolks and whisk well to combine. Whisk in the remaining ½ cup cold milk until smooth.) Attach the bowl to the mixer and fit the mixer with the paddle attachment.

2 On low speed, gradually add half of the flour and then the salt. Mix until a sticky, batter-like dough that clings to the sides of the bowl forms. Increase the speed to medium. Beat in half of the well-softened butter, 1 tablespoon at a time, letting each addition be absorbed before adding another. Replace the paddle attachment with the dough hook. Mix in half the remaining flour, then the remaining butter, and then the remaining flour, letting each addition be absorbed before adding the next. Knead on medium-low speed until the dough is smooth and soft, about 5 minutes.

3 Transfer the dough to a lightly floured work surface. Knead briefly to check the dough's texture: It should feel slightly sticky but not stick to the work surface. Knead in more flour only if needed. Generously butter a large bowl. Shape the dough into a taut ball. Place in the bowl, turn to coat with butter, and turn smooth side up. Cover tightly with plastic wrap. Let stand in a warm place until the dough doubles in volume, about 45 minutes.

4 Working carefully to preserve the dough's light and puffy texture, turn the dough out onto a lightly floured work surface. (Do not knead the dough.) Cut the dough in half and shape each piece into a 1-inch-thick rectangle. Cover with a kitchen towel and let rest for 15 minutes before using. If not using immediately, do not let the dough rest. Instead, immediately wrap each half tightly in plastic wrap and freeze for up to 2 weeks. To use the frozen dough, transfer to the refrigerator and let thaw for at least 8 hours, or up to overnight.

Ricotta and Marmalade Toasts

Makes 10 to 12 servings

This loaf looks like a pain de mie, but it has a far more tender crumb due to the generous amount of sour cream in the dough. Toasted slices taste like a cross between bread and pastry, making them ideal for a topping of creamy ricotta and a fruity spread.

SPECIAL EQUIPMENT: You can find 14 by 4 by 4-inch covered Pullman loaf pans in specialty cookware stores and online. If you don't want to buy one, you can bake the bread in a 9 by 5 by 3-inch loaf pan instead.

Softened unsalted butter, for the pan

½ recipe Yeasted Sour Cream Dough (page 152)

Unbleached all-purpose flour, for rolling the dough

High-quality ricotta cheese, for serving

Mandarin Orange Spread (page 176) or Apricot Spread (page 177), for serving

1 Lightly butter a 14 by 4 by 4-inch Pullman loaf pan, including the underside of the lid. Place the dough on a lightly floured work surface. Gently pressing to deflate the dough, roll it into a 15 by 8-inch rectangle with the long side facing you. To shape it into a loaf, fold in the right and left ends of the dough by about ½ inch and pinch the seams closed to form a 14 by 8-inch rectangle. Folding over one-third of the dough at a time, roll it up into a plump loaf, pressing the seam closed with the heel of your hand at every turn. Using your fingertips, pinch the final seam closed. Transfer the loaf, seam side down, to the pan, pressing down gently so it fits flat in the pan.

2 Cover the pan with the lid, leaving it open about 1 inch. Let stand in a warm place until the dough has risen to ½ inch below the edges of the pan, about 1 hour.

3 Position a rack in the center of the oven and preheat to 350°F.

4 Close the lid of the loaf pan completely. Bake until the top crust is golden brown, about 35 minutes. Do not underbake, or the loaf will collapse. Wearing oven mitts, you can very carefully slide open the top of the pan to see if the loaf is dark enough. If it's not, return the bread to the oven and bake, uncovered, until golden brown.

5 Let stand for 5 minutes, then remove the loaf from the pan. Transfer to a wire rack and let cool completely.

6 To serve, cut the bread into slices. Toast if desired. Spread ricotta on each toast and dollop the fruit spread on top.

Savory Spirals

Makes 16 spirals

Rolled up like croissants, these spirals bake into layers of moist, tender dough inside a golden brown crust. A light egg wash and a sprinkle of salt show off the savory side of my sour cream dough. These spirals would also make ideal dinner rolls.

Unbleached all-purpose flour, for rolling the dough
½ recipe Yeasted Sour Cream Dough (page 152)
1 large egg, well beaten
Kosher salt, for sprinkling

1 Line a half-sheet pan with parchment paper. Lightly dust a work surface with flour. Place the dough on the work surface and dust lightly with flour. Roll it out into an 18 by 12-inch rectangle, with a long side facing you.

2 Using a pizza wheel and a yardstick, neatly trim the rough edges of the dough. Cut the dough lengthwise in half to make two 18 by 6-inch rectangles. Starting at the top left corner of one rectangle, cut down to make a narrow triangle with a 1-inch base; set aside. Measure 2 inches from the top left corner of the rectangle and mark a notch with the wheel at this point. Cut down diagonally from the notch to meet the bottom left edge of the dough to make a triangle with a 2-inch base. Continue cutting, alternating diagonal cuts, to cut out 7 more triangles. The last cut will yield another narrow triangle with a 1-inch-wide base. Repeat with the second rectangle of dough to make 7 more large triangles and 2 narrow triangles, for a total of 14 large triangles and 4 narrow triangles.

3 Place a large triangle on the work surface with its base facing you. Stretch the bottom slightly so it is about 3½ inches wide. Pick up the triangle, holding the bottom of the triangle in one hand, and stretch it with your other hand until it is about 7 inches long. Return the triangle to the work surface. Starting at the bottom, roll up the triangle, finishing with the tip underneath the spiral. Place it tip side down on the pan. Repeat with the remaining large triangles, placing them 1½ inches apart on the pan. Then overlap 2 of the narrow triangles at their long sides, press the seam together, roll up as for the large triangles, and place on the pan. Repeat with the remaining 2 narrow triangles.

4 Choose a warm spot in the kitchen for proofing. Slip the pan with the spirals into a tall kitchen plastic bag. Place a tall glass of hot water on the pan to keep the bag from touching the dough. Wave the bag to inflate it and tightly close it, trapping air in the bag. Let stand until the spirals look puffy, about 40 minutes.

5 Position a rack in the center of the oven and preheat to 350°F.

6 Carefully remove the glass from the bag, then remove the pan with the spirals. Brush the tops of the spirals lightly all over with the beaten egg. Sprinkle with salt. Bake the spirals until the tops are golden brown, 15 to 18 minutes. Serve warm, or cool to room temperature.

Mini Pastry "Bagels"

Makes 1 dozen bagels

I'm a New Yorker, so I know I need to include this disclaimer: These are bagels in name only—because of their ring shape. They taste nothing like a real New York bagel. That being said, they're amazing when sandwiching classic bagel fillings. The hint of sweetness in the dough both complements fruit spreads and balances savory fillings like smoked fish; see the variation below.

Unbleached all-purpose flour, for rolling the dough

½ recipe Yeasted Sour Cream Dough (page 152)

Cream cheese, softened, for serving

Fruit preserves (pages 174 to 175), for serving

1 Line a half-sheet pan with parchment paper. Lightly dust a work surface with flour. Place the dough on the work surface and dust lightly with flour. Roll out the dough into a ½-inch-thick rectangle.

2 Using a 2½-inch biscuit cutter, cut out rounds from the dough. Gently press the scraps together (do not overhandle the dough) and repeat the rolling and cutting until you have 12 rounds. Using a 1-inch biscuit cutter, cut out a hole from the center of each round. Place the bagels and holes 1½ inches apart on the prepared pan.

3 Choose a warm spot in the kitchen for proofing. Slip the pan with the bagels and holes into a tall kitchen plastic bag. Place a tall glass of hot water on the pan to keep the bag from touching the dough. Wave the bag to inflate it and tightly close it, trapping air in the bag. Let stand until the bagels and holes look puffy, about 30 minutes.

4 Position a rack in the center of the oven and preheat to 350°F.

5 Carefully remove the glass from the bag, then remove the pan. Bake the bagels and holes until the tops are golden brown, about 13 minutes. Cool to warm or room temperature.

6 To serve, slice each bagel and hole in half, spread with cream cheese and preserves, and sandwich together.

Smoked Fish and Cream Cheese "Bagels": Substitute flaked skinned and boned smoked trout or sliced smoked salmon for the preserves. If desired, top with sliced tomatoes, sliced red onion, and capers and serve with lemon wedges or caper berries (photo opposite).

Honey-Pecan Sticky Buns

Makes 1 dozen sticky buns

For the perfect proportion of caramelized crust to buttery bun, I bake these in muffin tins. When I flip out the buns, each gets its own cascade of pecans and honeyed caramel down its burnished browned sides. I advise you to let these cool for at least a bit so you don't burn your mouth, but even I have trouble waiting to dive into them.

Goop

14 tablespoons (198 grams) unsalted butter, chilled and cut into ½-inch cubes

¼ cup plus 3 tablespoons (86 grams) superfine sugar

¼ cup plus 3 tablespoons (86 grams) packed light brown sugar

⅓ cup (113 grams) light clover or orange blossom honey

1 tablespoon superfine sugar

¼ teaspoon ground cinnamon

Unbleached all-purpose flour, for rolling the dough

½ recipe Yeasted Sour Cream Dough (page 152)

3 tablespoons unsalted butter, well softened

½ cup (74 grams) currants

2 cups (220 grams) chopped pecans

Softened unsalted butter, for the pan

1 To make the goop: In the bowl of a heavy-duty stand mixer fitted with the paddle attachment, beat the butter on high speed until smooth, about 1 minute. Gradually add the superfine sugar and then the brown sugar, reduce the speed to medium, and beat until creamy. Scrape down the sides of the bowl with a silicone spatula. Add the honey and beat on medium speed just until well blended; do not overbeat. Set aside.

2 In a small bowl, mix the sugar and cinnamon; set aside.

3 Lightly dust a work surface with flour. Place the dough on the work surface and dust lightly with flour. Roll out the dough into an 18 by 10-inch rectangle, with a long side facing you. Brush the well-softened butter over the surface, leaving a ½-inch border on all sides. Sprinkle the currants and 1 cup pecans over the butter, then sprinkle with the cinnamon sugar.

4 Starting at the top, fold in and press down 1 inch of dough, then tightly roll up the dough. Pinch the seam closed. Roll the dough back and forth underneath your palms to seal the seam securely. Push the ends in on each side and roll again to stretch the log to 18 inches.

5 Brush the insides of 12 muffin cups with softened butter, then brush the top of the tin. Divide the goop evenly among the muffin cups and press it into the bottoms with your fingers. Sprinkle the remaining 1 cup

pecans over the goop. Use a sharp knife to cut the dough into 12 even (1½-inch) pieces. Press the buns cut side down into the cups; the top of the dough should be flush with the top of the pan. Place the muffin tin on a half-sheet pan.

6 Choose a warm spot in the kitchen for proofing. Slip the pan with the muffin tin into a tall kitchen plastic bag. Place one tall glass of hot water on either side of the muffin tin to keep the bag from touching the dough. Wave the bag to inflate it and tightly close it, trapping air in the bag. Let stand until the buns rise 1 inch above the rim of the pan, about 40 minutes.

7 Position a rack in the center of the oven and preheat to 350°F.

8 Carefully remove the glasses from the bag, then remove the tin. Bake the buns in the tin on the half-sheet pan, to catch any drips, until the tops are golden brown and the bottoms are caramelized, about 30 minutes.

9 Cool the buns in the tin on a wire rack for 5 minutes. Butter a half-sheet pan and center it over the muffin tin. Wearing oven mitts, grip the pan and tin together and quickly but carefully flip both over. Lift off the muffin tin. Transfer the sticky buns to a serving dish and spoon any pecans and caramel left in the muffin tin or half-sheet pan over them. Serve warm.

Amma's Hungarian Coffee Cake

Makes 1 loaf

My daughters go crazy every time I make this cake. It was a specialty of their grandmother, whom they called "Amma." Here, I've tried to re-create it exactly as I remember it. Although bordering on bread-like, this cake still tastes like a sweet treat, with its streusel topping. I use a babka rolling technique here so that the cinnamon sugar spirals all throughout the twists and turns of the soft dough.

Streusel

⅓ cup (47 grams) unbleached all-purpose flour
1 tablespoon superfine sugar
1 tablespoon packed light brown sugar
⅛ teaspoon ground cinnamon
Pinch of fine sea salt
2 tablespoons unsalted butter, melted and cooled

⅓ cup (65 grams) packed light brown sugar
2 tablespoons superfine sugar
1½ teaspoons ground cinnamon
Unbleached all-purpose flour, for rolling the dough
½ recipe Yeasted Sour Cream Dough (page 152)
4 tablespoons (57 grams) unsalted butter, well softened
1 large egg, well beaten
Softened unsalted butter, for the pan and brushing the dough

1 To make the streusel: In a small bowl, mix the flour, superfine sugar, brown sugar, cinnamon, salt, and butter with your fingers until combined and crumbly. Set aside.

2 In another small bowl, mix the brown sugar, superfine sugar, and cinnamon; set aside.

3 Lightly dust a work surface with flour. Place the dough on the work surface and dust lightly with flour. Roll out the dough into an 18 by 10-inch rectangle, with a long side facing you. Brush the well-softened butter over the surface, leaving a 1-inch border on all sides. Sprinkle the sugar mixture over the butter.

4 Starting at the top, tightly roll up the dough. Brush the empty border of dough with the beaten egg and pinch the seam closed. Roll the dough back and forth underneath your palms to seal the seam securely. Push the ends in on each side and roll again to stretch the log to 18 inches. Fold the dough roughly in half to form a U-shaped curve, with one side 3 inches longer than the other. Using the side of your hand, press a dent into

the dough at its bend. Fold the longer length of dough over and around the shorter length twice to make two humps. Twist the dough lengths to create a third hump and tuck the two ends under the loaf. You should have a loaf about 9 inches long with 3 humps.

5 Generously butter a 9 by 5 by 3-inch loaf pan. Transfer the dough to the pan, being sure that the ends are well secured under it. Gently brush the softened butter all over the top of the dough. Sprinkle the streusel over the top, patting gently so it adheres. (Don't worry if some of the streusel falls into the corners or sides of the pan.) Place the loaf pan on a half-sheet pan.

6 Choose a warm spot in the kitchen for proofing. Slip the pan with the loaf pan into a tall kitchen plastic bag. Place a tall glass of hot water on either side of the loaf pan to keep the bag from touching the dough. Wave the bag to inflate it and tightly close it, trapping air in the bag. Let stand until the loaf rises 2½ inches above the rim of the pan, about 45 minutes.

7 Position a rack in the center of the oven and preheat to 350°F.

8 Carefully remove the glasses from the bag, then remove the pan. Bake the cake on the half-sheet pan until the top is deep golden brown, the dough in the crevices looks fully baked, and an instant-read thermometer inserted into the center of the cake reads at least 195°F, 45 to 50 minutes. If the loaf threatens to burn, cover the top loosely with foil.

9 Cool in the pan on a wire rack for 10 minutes. Carefully unmold the cake onto the rack and let cool completely right side up.

10 To serve, slice the cake with a serrated knife.

Chapter Seven

Sauces, Spreads, Preserves, and Pickles

I'VE BUILT MY CAREER ON "LEGENDARY SPREADS" BECAUSE I TRULY BELIEVE THAT A FINISHING TOUCH MAKES ANY DISH INFINITELY BETTER. A DRIZZLE of homemade syrup or sauce, a smear of a fruit spread or flavored butter, or a layer of pickles will turn an already delicious dish into a truly spectacular one. This applies to both sweet and savory meals, and it is especially true at breakfast. In fact, I think of condiments as the bridge between sweet and salty, and the recipes in this chapter bring those two worlds together.

Because they should be used sparingly, condiments need to be full-flavored. They're intended to enhance main dishes, not overpower them. Sauces, syrups, and jams should be sweet, butters should taste bold, and pickles should bring a briny punch. Less is definitely more when topping off a dish. Don't turn your breakfast into a plate of syrup with a side order of waffles or pancakes.

Since you usually add condiments to taste as you're eating, you can mix and match flavors to see what you like best. With a stash of from-scratch condiments on hand, you can create your own unique meals.

KEY INGREDIENTS

Lemons: A hit of lemon juice not only brightens fruit flavors, it also helps preserves set. Keep a fresh supply on hand—make sure they are firm and heavy for their size.

Vinegar: I make my pickles with vinegar to infuse them quickly with tartness. Different brands vary in their sourness, so you may want to taste your pickling solution and adjust the vinegar or sugar as needed.

TOOL KIT

Canning Jars: Glass jars with lids are necessary for keeping preserves and pickles, and they are also handy for storing any condiments. They don't absorb odors and, in turn, release strong aromas the way plastic containers can. Some jars are even pretty enough to go from the fridge to the table.

Heavy Nonreactive Saucepan: A sturdy heavy-bottomed saucepan will ensure that sauces, syrups, and fruit spreads don't scorch. You don't want the taste of burned sugar! Don't use a pan made from untreated aluminum, which can react with acids and give the preserves a metallic flavor—make sure the interior of the pan is nonreactive.

SYRUPS AND SAUCES

I love maple syrup. I love it even more when it's infused with fresh seasonal fruit. Of course, I also adore fruit sauces of all types that highlight the best produce. The uses for these sauces are endless: Drizzle or spoon over any type of griddle cake, waffles, French toast, biscuits, scones, muffins, cakes, even ice cream. They're all very easy to make but will really impress at the breakfast table. Prepare a selection and show off their stunning hues in clear serving vessels.

Apple Maple Syrup

Makes about 1½ cups

Green apples and maple syrup are a delicious combination—the apples mellow the sweetness of the syrup and pick up a delightful maple flavor at the same time.

1 cup (292 grams) pure maple syrup

1 medium tart green apple, such as Granny Smith (8 ounces; 227 grams), peeled, cored, and shredded

1½ teaspoons fresh lemon juice

Seeds from ½ vanilla bean, preferably a Plumped Vanilla Bean (page 3), or ½ teaspoon pure vanilla extract

1 In a small saucepan, heat the syrup just to a simmer over low heat. Remove from the heat and stir in the apple, lemon juice, and vanilla seeds. Cover and let stand for at least 2 hours to meld the flavors.

2 The syrup can be covered and refrigerated for up to 2 days. Serve at room temperature or reheat gently to remove its chill.

Raspberry Maple Syrup

Makes about 2 cups

The raspberries will become plump and juicy with the syrup. If you'd prefer a smooth, runny syrup, puree the soaked raspberries and syrup in a food processor or blender and strain.

½ pint (6 ounces; 170 grams) raspberries • 1 cup (292 grams) pure maple syrup

1 In a pint container with a tight-fitting lid, combine the raspberries and maple syrup. Cover and refrigerate for at least 3 days, or up to 1 week.

2 Serve the syrup at room temperature.

Bumpy Blueberry Sauce

Makes about 3 cups

A gem-colored sauce that never fails to please.

2 pints (1½ pounds; 680 grams) blueberries

2 tablespoons fresh lemon juice

1 cup (200 grams) granulated sugar

1 In a nonreactive medium saucepan, combine the blueberries and lemon juice and bring to a simmer over medium heat. Reduce the heat to low and cook, stirring occasionally, until the berries are tender and juicy, about 10 minutes.

2 Stir in the sugar and cook, stirring occasionally, until the sauce is slightly thickened but some whole berries remain, about 10 minutes. Serve warm, or cool completely and refrigerate in an airtight container for up to 1 week. Reheat gently before serving.

Strawberry-Raspberry Sauce

Makes about 3 cups

These delicious berries should be prepared at least 2 hours before serving so they will release their juices, but the sauce is best when eaten within 12 hours.

1 pint (12 ounces; 340 grams) strawberries, hulled and sliced

½ pint (6 ounces; 170 grams) raspberries

1 cup (196 grams) superfine sugar

1 tablespoon fresh lemon juice

Seeds from ½ vanilla bean, preferably a Plumped Vanilla Bean (page 3), or ½ teaspoon pure vanilla extract

1 In a medium bowl, gently combine the strawberries, raspberries, sugar, lemon juice, and vanilla seeds. Cover with plastic wrap and let stand, stirring occasionally, until the fruit has given off its juices, about 2 hours.

2 The sauce can be covered and refrigerated for up to 12 hours. Bring to room temperature before serving.

Meyer Lemon Curd

Makes about 1 cup

Meyer lemons used to be available only from specialty stores; now you can find them in supermarkets during their winter season. Their aromatic zest and tart juice have a rounded tangerine-orange note. They make the most tempting lemon curd, which you can dollop on toast, biscuits, scones, muffins, waffles, or just about anything on the breakfast table. Mixed with maple syrup, the curd becomes an unbelievable pancake topper.

2 large Meyer lemons

5 large egg yolks

½ cup (98 grams) superfine sugar

4 tablespoons (57 grams) unsalted butter, cut into ½-inch cubes, at room temperature

1 Rinse the lemons under cold water and dry well. Zest the lemons into a heatproof medium bowl or the top of a double boiler, being sure to avoid the bitter white pith. Halve the lemons and squeeze the juice into a strainer set over a liquid measuring cup. You should have about ⅓ cup juice. Add the juice, egg yolks, and sugar to the zest and whisk to combine.

2 Place a medium-mesh sieve over another heatproof medium bowl near the stove. Set the bowl with the lemon mixture over a saucepan of simmering water or the bottom of a double boiler. Cook the mixture, using a silicone spatula to scrape down the sides of the bowl often, until it is opaque and thick enough to cling to the spatula, about 10 minutes. (A finger run through the mixture on the spatula should cut a swath, and an instant-read thermometer inserted into the mixture should register 185°F.)

3 Strain the mixture through the sieve into the bowl: Use the spatula to stir the mixture to help it flow through the sieve and gently push it through the strainer; don't force any solids into the bowl. Gradually whisk in the butter, allowing each addition to be incorporated before adding more.

4 Press a piece of plastic wrap directly onto the surface of the curd and pierce a few holes in it to allow steam to escape. Cool completely, then transfer to a covered container and refrigerate until cold. The curd can be refrigerated in an airtight container for up to 3 days.

Meyer Lemon Maple Syrup: Whisk ¼ cup (70 grams) Meyer Lemon Curd into 2 cups (584 grams) pure maple syrup until well combined.

Sweet Butters

SPREAD TOASTED HOMEMADE BREAD (PAGES 138 TO 146) WITH ONE OF THESE SIMPLE BLENDS TO MAKE YOUR MORNING REALLY SPECIAL. EACH ONE MAKES ABOUT ⅔ CUP, WHICH FITS nicely into a 6-ounce ramekin. If you smooth the top with an offset spatula, you can use the tines of a fork to inscribe your initials or another design. The butters can be tightly covered and refrigerated for up to 3 days.

Jam Butter: In a medium bowl, mash 8 tablespoons (114 grams) room-temperature unsalted butter with 3 tablespoons preserves (pages 174 to 175) or jam (pages 178 to 180) until well combined and smooth.

Honey-Pecan Butter: In a medium bowl, mash 8 tablespoons (114 grams) room-temperature unsalted butter with 2 tablespoons honey until well combined and smooth. Fold in 2 tablespoons finely chopped toasted pecans (page 41) until evenly distributed.

Meyer Lemon Curd Butter: In a medium bowl, mash 8 tablespoons (114 grams) room-temperature unsalted butter with 3 tablespoons Meyer Lemon Curd (page 169) until well combined and smooth.

Maple-Sea Salt Butter: In a medium bowl, mash 8 tablespoons (114 grams) room-temperature unsalted butter with 2 tablespoons pure maple syrup until well combined and smooth. Transfer to a ramekin, smooth the top, and sprinkle with coarse sea salt, such as Maldon, Himalayan pink, or fleur de sel.

Goat Cheese Spread

Makes about ¾ cup

Goat cheese adds a complex tang to a classic herbed cream cheese spread. This tastes especially good with any smoked fish. I also like it in a sandwich with tomatoes and cucumbers or simply spread on Mini Pastry "Bagels" (page 156), Cornbread (page 47), or toast.

4 ounces (114 grams) fresh goat cheese, softened
4 ounces (114 grams) cream cheese, softened
1 teaspoon minced fresh dill
½ teaspoon very finely chopped fresh chives
Kosher salt

In a medium bowl, mash the goat cheese and cream cheese together with a silicone spatula until well combined and smooth. Fold in the dill and chives until evenly distributed. Transfer to a serving dish and smooth the top with an offset spatula. Sprinkle the top with salt. The spread can be refrigerated in an airtight container for up to 3 days.

FRUIT SPREADS

I consider myself an expert on homemade jams, but sometimes even I don't have the tools at hand to can jars of freshly simmered fruit spreads. Recently, we completely renovated our home. My canning pots and tools were all packed away during the process, so I couldn't seal jam jars. That's when I turned to small-batch refrigerator jams. They cook very quickly and don't need to be canned. They don't last very long in the refrigerator, but they all got eaten in my home long before their end date.

Refrigerator jams require little planning and effort and result in lots of pleasure. Toast is the obvious base for spreading, but fruit spreads can also surprise in savory dishes like omelets (page 199). Almost any breakfast dish benefits from a little smear of homemade jam.

TIPS FOR PERFECT REFRIGERATOR FRUIT SPREADS

1 Get set up before you start cooking. Even though you will not be heat-sealing the jars, you still need high-quality glass jars and new lids. Wash the jars, lids, and bands in hot soapy water and rinse them well. If you wish, you can use the dishwasher, but don't put the lids in it; wash them separately by hand. You'll also need a thick towel to place the jars on after they're filled. Jars filled with hot jam can crack if set on a cold surface.

2 Taste your fruit before you start cooking. If it's very sweet, reduce the amount of sugar to taste. Because sugar acts as a preservative, the more sugar you add, the longer the preserves will last, but these small batches will go fast either way.

3 Don't overcook the fruit-sugar mixture. When preserving fruits, the goal is to capture the flavor of the fruit. I like a jam that's a bit runny. As long as the spread doesn't cross over the line into a syrup, the thickness is not as important as the flavor. And remember, the jam firms up as it cools.

4 Get the fruit spreads securely into the jars. A canning funnel helps but isn't necessary. Leave ¼-inch head-space at the tops of the jars and wipe the rims clean with a hot wet towel. Gently poke through the spread to the bottom of the jar with a butter knife to release any air pockets. Put on the hot wet lids and screw on the bands.

5 Let the spreads cool completely at room temperature before transferring to the refrigerator. Again, the hot jars could crack if shocked with cold.

6 Serve within 2 weeks. When serving, never put used spoons or butter knives into the jars. This can create bacteria and spoil your beautiful spreads.

Plum Preserves

Makes about 3 half-pints

For nice, tart preserves, start with nice, tart fruit. Here I combine three popular varieties of plums, but you should taste different heirloom plum options at your local market. Just be sure to use a total of 3½ packed cups cut plums. And although you want flavorful, ripe fruit, it's better for them to be a little hard than a little soft.

2 black plums (8 ounces; 227 grams), halved, pitted, and cut into ½-inch dice (1½ cups)

1 red plum (5 ounces; 142 grams), halved, pitted, and cut into ½-inch dice (1 cup)

2 pluots (6 ounces; 170 grams), halved, pitted, and cut into ½-inch dice (1 cup)

¼ cup (56 grams) water

1 tablespoon fresh lemon juice

1 cup (200 grams) granulated sugar

1 In a nonreactive large saucepan, bring the black and red plums, the pluots, water, and lemon juice to a simmer over medium heat, stirring occasionally. Reduce the heat to low and simmer, stirring occasionally, until the fruit starts to soften but some chunks remain intact, about 3 minutes.

2 Stir in the sugar. Continue simmering, stirring occasionally, until the preserves are thickened but still soupy, about 10 minutes. Skim off and discard any foam on the surface.

3 Divide the preserves among three clean half-pint canning jars. Seal and cool to room temperature, then refrigerate for up to 2 weeks.

Plum Ketchup: In a nonreactive large saucepan, bring 1 cup (308 grams) Plum Preserves, ¼ cup (56 grams) red wine, and 2 tablespoons red wine vinegar to a boil over medium heat, stirring often. Reduce the heat to medium-low and simmer for 5 minutes. Transfer to a blender, add 1 cup (240 grams) ketchup, and puree until smooth. Transfer to a medium bowl and stir in another 1 cup (240 grams) ketchup. Season to taste with freshly ground black pepper. The ketchup can be covered and refrigerated for up to 1 month. Makes about 3 cups.

Strawberry-Rhubarb Preserves

Makes about 2 half-pints

One of spring's most beloved combinations becomes even more delicious with the addition of lemon and a vanilla bean. I use whole lemon slices, rind and all. The rind provides both extra pectin to help the preserves set and lovely bits to chew on. The speckles of vanilla seeds turn this into a stunner and add an aroma that makes you feel like you're eating dessert.

1½ stalks rhubarb (8 ounces; 227 grams), tough strings removed with a vegetable peeler, stalks cut into ¼-inch slices (1¼ cups)

7 strawberries (8 ounces; 227 grams), hulled, quartered lengthwise, and cut crosswise into ½-inch-thick slices (1⅓ cups)

½ Meyer lemon or ¼ regular lemon (1½ ounces; 42 grams), cut into ⅛-inch-thick slices and seeded

¼ cup (56 grams) water

1½ cups (300 grams) granulated sugar

½ vanilla bean, preferably a Plumped Vanilla Bean (page 3)

1 In a nonreactive large saucepan, bring the rhubarb, strawberries, lemon, and water to a simmer over medium heat, stirring occasionally. Reduce the heat to medium-low and simmer for 5 minutes, stirring occasionally.

2 Stir in the sugar. Using the tip of a knife, split the half vanilla bean and scrape the seeds into the mixture (or, if using a plumped vanilla bean, squeeze out the seeds); add the pod. Continue simmering, stirring occasionally, until the preserves are thickened, about 10 minutes. Skim off and discard any foam on the surface. Discard the vanilla pod.

3 Divide the jam between two clean half-pint canning jars. Seal and cool to room temperature, then refrigerate for up to 2 weeks.

Mandarin Orange Spread

Makes about 2 half-pints

From-scratch spreads can require extra care. In this case, I peel off every white string from the oranges before separating the segments and cutting each one lengthwise in half. I do it for a reason. Golden Nugget mandarin oranges taste like a burst of sunshine, and I wanted to capture their juicy, complex citrus sweetness in a jar without any hint of bitterness from the white pith. Slicing the segments exposes more of their flesh, so they cook quickly. Overcooking will compromise their freshness.

14 seedless mandarin oranges, preferably Golden Nugget, peeled and white strings removed (10¾ ounces; 305 grams)

1 tablespoon fresh lemon juice

1½ cups (300 grams) granulated sugar

1 Separate the oranges into segments, removing any remaining white strings. You should have 4 cups packed segments. Cut each segment lengthwise in half.

2 In a nonreactive large saucepan, bring the orange segments and lemon juice to a simmer over medium heat, stirring occasionally. Reduce the heat to medium-low and simmer, stirring occasionally, until the fruit breaks down and releases its juices, about 5 minutes.

3 Stir in the sugar. Continue simmering, stirring occasionally, until the spread is slightly thickened, about 5 minutes.

4 Using an immersion (stick) blender or a stand blender, carefully puree the mixture until almost smooth (return it to the saucepan if you used a stand blender). Bring to a boil over medium-high heat, then reduce the heat to maintain a steady simmer and simmer until the spread is thickened, about 5 minutes. Skim off and discard any foam on the surface.

5 Divide the spread between two clean half-pint canning jars. Seal and cool to room temperature, then refrigerate for up to 2 weeks.

Apricot Spread

Makes about 2 half-pints

Golden Velvet apricots, so named because their skins feel amazingly velvety, have all the complexity of regular apricots but with a more subtle tartness. Combined with regular large apricots, they simmer into an irresistible golden jam.

2 very large apricots (10 ounces; 283 grams), halved, pitted, and cut into ½-inch dice (1½ cups)

6 small Golden Velvet apricots (10 ounces; 283 grams), halved, pitted, and cut into ½-inch dice (1 cup)

¼ cup (56 grams) water

1 tablespoon fresh lemon juice

1¼ cups (250 grams) granulated sugar

¼ teaspoon pure almond extract

1 In a nonreactive large saucepan, bring the large and small apricots, water, and lemon juice to a simmer over medium heat, stirring occasionally. Reduce the heat to low and simmer, stirring occasionally, until the fruit starts to soften but some chunks remain intact, about 5 minutes.

2 Stir in the sugar and almond extract. Continue simmering, stirring occasionally, until the spread is thickened, about 15 minutes. Skim off and discard any foam on the surface.

3 Divide the spread between two clean half-pint canning jars. Seal and cool to room temperature, then refrigerate for up to 2 weeks.

Strawberry Jam

Makes about 2 half-pints

Years ago, when I made my very first batch of strawberry jam, I learned that the fruit will never set without added pectin. I had flats and flats of berries from a pick-your-own farm and I was so excited to capture the flavor of in-season berries. The strawberries were so fresh, their intense heady aroma almost induced a nearly asthmatic reaction. Although my jam tasted great, I hadn't added any pectin, and it never set. Since that experience, I always add natural sources of pectin. Here I combine lemon and orange juice, which gel the jam and heighten the berries' sweetness.

1¼ pounds (567 grams) strawberries, hulled and cut into ½-inch chunks (3 cups)

¼ cup (56 grams) fresh orange juice

2 tablespoons fresh lemon juice

1½ cups (300 grams) granulated sugar

1 In a nonreactive large saucepan, bring the strawberries, orange juice, and lemon juice to a simmer over medium heat, stirring occasionally. Reduce the heat to medium-low and simmer for 5 minutes, stirring occasionally.

2 Stir in the sugar. Continue simmering, stirring occasionally, until the jam is thickened and the juices are translucent, about 15 minutes. Skim off and discard any foam on the surface.

3 Divide the jam between two clean half-pint canning jars. Seal and cool to room temperature, then refrigerate for up to 2 weeks.

Blueberry-Blackberry Jam

Makes about 3 half-pints

The natural pectin in these dark berries turns the cooking process into pure pleasure: I love pulling my spoon through the lava-like mixture and watching the bubbles ripple with each stir. And I love eating it just as much.

2 cups (12 ounces; 340 grams) blackberries

2 cups (10 ounces; 283 grams) blueberries

1 tablespoon plus 1 teaspoon fresh lemon juice

1½ cups (300 grams) granulated sugar

½ vanilla bean, preferably a Plumped Vanilla Bean (page 3)

1 In a nonreactive large saucepan, bring the blackberries, blueberries, and lemon juice to a simmer over medium heat, stirring occasionally. Reduce the heat to medium-low and simmer for 8 minutes, stirring occasionally.

2 Stir in the sugar. Using the tip of a knife, split the half vanilla bean and scrape the seeds into the mixture (or, if using a plumped vanilla bean, squeeze out the seeds); add the pod. Continue simmering, stirring occasionally, until the jam is thickened, about 8 minutes. Skim off and discard any foam on the surface. Discard the vanilla pod.

3 Divide the jam among three clean half-pint canning jars. Seal and cool to room temperature, then refrigerate for up to 2 weeks.

Three-Berry Jam: Substitute 1 cup raspberries for 1 cup of the blueberries or blackberries.

Fig Jam

Makes about 2 half-pints

Every fall, I get my hands on as many fresh figs as I can. In fact, I have a friend with a huge fig tree in her backyard in Brooklyn. Lucky me. Those figs make the most flavorful jam—their deep garnet color is unforgettable.

COOK'S NOTE: If you're starting with really ripe figs that already taste jam-like, be sure to reduce the sugar to taste.

11 ounces (312 grams) fresh figs, trimmed and diced (2 cups)

2 tablespoons water

2 tablespoons fresh orange juice

1 tablespoon fresh lemon juice

1 cup (200 grams) granulated sugar

1 In a nonreactive large saucepan, bring the figs, water, orange juice, and lemon juice to a simmer over medium heat, stirring occasionally. Reduce the heat to medium-low and simmer for 5 minutes, stirring occasionally.

2 Stir in the sugar. Continue simmering, stirring occasionally, until the figs are completely soft, about 15 minutes. Skim off and discard any foam on the surface.

3 Divide the jam between two clean half-pint canning jars. Seal and cool to room temperature, then refrigerate for up to 2 weeks.

Chunky Apple Butter

Make about 3 cups

There's no butter in apple butter. Its name reflects its rich, luscious texture, which comes from simmering apples in juice, and its versatility as a spread. Apple butters are often smooth, but I prefer mine a little chunky.

2 pounds (908 grams) Granny Smith apples, peeled, cored, and cut into ½-inch dice

½ cup (112 grams) unsweetened apple juice

1½ tablespoons fresh lemon juice

¼ teaspoon ground cinnamon

1½ cups (300 grams) granulated sugar

½ vanilla bean, preferably a Plumped Vanilla Bean (page 3)

1 In a nonreactive large saucepan, bring the apples, apple juice, lemon juice, and cinnamon to a simmer over medium heat, stirring often. Reduce the heat to medium-low and simmer, stirring often, until the apples are barely tender, about 10 minutes.

2 Stir in the sugar. Using the tip of a knife, split the half vanilla bean and scrape the seeds into the mixture (or, if using a plumped vanilla bean, squeeze out the seeds); add the pod. Bring to a simmer over medium heat, then reduce the heat to maintain a steady simmer and cook, stirring often, until the apples have broken down into a thick, chunky puree, about 25 minutes. Discard the vanilla pod.

3 Transfer the apple butter to an airtight container and refrigerate for up to 1 week.

PICKLES

Sweet and salty may rule the day in condiments, but sour enhances dishes too. I adore pickles and enjoy them straight from the jar. They're also wonderful for balancing the richness of breakfast meats such as sausage and brightening fresh vegetables. Of course they can make an appearance at any time of day. Thin slices work well in sandwiches, while julienned pickles can be sprinkled on main dishes. As with my refrigerator preserves, I make small batches of pickles, skip the canning process, and store them in jars in the refrigerator for up to a month.

Bread-and-Butter Pickles

Makes about 2 cups

Whenever I open a jar of these gorgeous green pickle slices, I can't stop snacking on them. They hit a sweet-and-sour balance that makes them irresistible. I created them to slip into the Herbed-Sausage Breakfast Sliders (page 246) and the Ham and Cheese Turnovers (page 237), where they complement the salty richness of the pork.

1 cup (224 grams) rice wine vinegar
1 cup (224 grams) water
1 cup (200 grams) granulated sugar
2 cups (218 grams) very thinly sliced Kirby cucumbers

1 In a nonreactive medium saucepan, combine the vinegar, water, and sugar. Bring to a boil, stirring to dissolve the sugar.

2 Meanwhile, put the cucumber slices in a nonreactive medium airtight container. Pour the hot pickling liquid over the cucumbers and cover tightly. Cool to room temperature, then refrigerate at least overnight, or for up to 1 month.

Bloody Mary Pickles

Makes about 4 cups

These are the crown jewels of our restaurant's signature brunch cocktail, the Crunchy No-Booze Bloody Mary (page 21). Their tart crunch completely transforms the familiar drink. This recipe makes a lot, because the more pickles in a Bloody Mary, the better. If you have any left over, sprinkle them over Roasted Chicken and Fennel Patties (page 250) or Three-Herb Gravlax (page 254), or simply set them out as a great little nibble.

2 cups (448 grams) apple cider vinegar

2 cups (448 grams) water

¾ cup (150 grams) granulated sugar

¾ teaspoon fine sea salt

3½ ounces (100 grams) celery, strings removed with a vegetable peeler, cut into 3-inch lengths and julienned (1 cup)

4½ ounces (127 grams) carrots, peeled, cut into 3-inch lengths and julienned (1 cup)

3½ ounces (100 grams) red bell pepper, cut into 3-inch lengths and julienned (1 cup) (see Cook's Note on page 241)

4 ounces (114 grams) jicama, cut into 3-inch lengths and julienned (1 cup)

1 In a nonreactive medium saucepan, combine the vinegar, water, sugar, and salt. Bring to a boil, stirring to dissolve the sugar.

2 Meanwhile, in a nonreactive large airtight container, combine the celery, carrots, bell peppers, and jicama. Pour the hot pickling liquid over the vegetables and cover tightly. Cool to room temperature, then refrigerate at least overnight, or for up to 1 month.

Vitamin A 6% • Vitamin C 0%
Calcium 2% • Iron 4%

Chapter Eight

Eggs Every Way

FOR MANY YEARS, I WAS AT THE STOVE DURING THE HECTIC BRUNCH SHIFTS AT OUR RESTAURANTS. THERE'S NO BETTER PLACE TO LEARN ABOUT wide-ranging egg-eating habits. Orders would fly in: "Sunny-side up, but with a little frizzled brown around the edges." "Soft, but not too soft." "Just a little runny." When I surveyed the dining rooms, I'd see some customers mashing their scrambled eggs with a fork, others scooping the eggs onto toast to make a sandwich. Fried eggs were most often eaten in three styles: cut-everything-up-all-together-before-eating, cut-the-yolk-out-first, or leave-out-the-yolk. I've seen diners crumble up toast to stir into their soft-boiled eggs and purists who spoon the eggs directly from the shell. I've observed some diners cutting plain omelets into strips and dolloping them with jam and others eating all of the filling but only a bit of the eggs. ("I wanted a one-egg omelet, so I ate only one egg's worth." Makes sense to me.)

Although I'm no longer cooking on the line, I still marvel at the many different ways eggs get from plate to mouth. My family members eat their eggs in different ways, as do my friends. No matter what the fork-and-knife strategy, though, the key to enjoying a good egg dish is to start with perfectly prepared eggs. In the recipes that follow, I show you how to make the most of everyone's favorite breakfast ingredient.

KEY INGREDIENT

Eggs: At our restaurants, eggs are delivered fresh from the most reliable nearby farmer. At home, I buy organic, local, and sustainably raised eggs from farmers' markets, supermarkets, or natural food stores. They are simply better tasting and handled with more care than factory eggs. Look for the freshest eggs by comparing best-by dates. Refrigerate eggs in their carton—never store them at room temperature or in the egg holders on some refrigerator doors, which can be the warmest spot in the refrigerator. Leaving the eggs in their carton also helps keep unwanted odors from seeping into them through their porous shells.

The fear of eating undercooked eggs has diminished in recent years, but it certainly still exists. It is true that in rare cases eggs may contain the harmful salmonella bacterium. In order to kill it, eggs must be cooked to above 170°F. However, skillet-cooked eggs cooked to this temperature will be rubbery and tough. If you don't care for well-done eggs (I certainly do not), it is important to take a few precautions. Although they won't kill salmonella, they will reduce the risk. You can also purchase pasteurized eggs, which have been heat-treated to reduce the risk of food-borne illnesses. If you wish, wash the shells with very mild soapy water, being sure to rinse and dry them well. But don't do this until just before using, or you'll remove the natural coating that keeps the eggs sealed and fresh. Never use cracked eggs. Avoid serving undercooked eggs to the elderly, the very young, or pregnant women, or to any person who has a compromised or impaired immune system. Wash your hands, utensils, and any cooking area that may have come into contact with raw eggs well with hot soapy water.

TOOL KIT

Nonstick Skillet: It is important to use a high-quality nonstick pan. For the best heat distribution, it should be on the heavy side with a thick bottom. A pan for omelets should have sloping sides so the omelets will slide out easily. For both scrambled eggs and omelets, an 8½-inch skillet is the perfect size. (For fried eggs, you may want a larger one for bigger batches.) Once you have the right pan, reserve it for eggs only. Be kind to your pan, and avoid scratching it. Eggs will stick to damaged nonstick pans. Use appropriate utensils, such as heatproof silicone spatulas and wooden spoons, and only the cleansers recommended by the manufacturer.

Immersion (Stick) Blender: This small appliance is the best tool for blending eggs for omelets and scrambled eggs to make them perfectly smooth when cooked. Even with vigorous hand-whisking, you'll never be able to incorporate the chalazae, those thick white cords attached to the yolk. The blender does the job in a couple of seconds.

Fine-Mesh Sieve: To get your omelets and scrambled eggs restaurant-level smooth, you can strain the blended eggs through a sieve. It has the added benefit of catching any bits of shell that may have fallen into the mix.

TIPS FOR PERFECT EGGS

1 All egg dishes should be made with room-temperature eggs. Extreme temperature changes from cold to hot can crack the shells of eggs that are hard- or soft-boiled and make the yolks of sunny-side-up eggs break. Remove eggs from the refrigerator at least 1 hour before cooking. If you forget, place the unshelled eggs in a bowl, cover with lukewarm water, and let stand for a few minutes to remove the chill.

2 Moderate heat and clarified butter combine to give superior results when cooking eggs. Heat the butter in the pan over medium-high heat just until it is hot. After you add the eggs, reduce the heat to low. This is especially important with omelets and scrambled eggs—slow, even cooking will give you creamy eggs with a soft texture. If the heat is too high, those tender eggs will turn to rubber.

3 I don't like streaks of whites in my scrambled eggs or omelets. Eggs should always be well beaten with an immersion (stick) blender, which can be inserted right into the bowl to quickly whirl the eggs into a homogenous golden mass.

4 At the restaurants, we force the beaten eggs through a cone-shaped wire-mesh strainer (chinois) to remove the tiny white cords called chalazae. At home, when you are cooking just a few eggs, the chalazae won't get in the way. But if you are beating a dozen eggs or more for a large batch of omelets, some omelets may end up with more than their share of the tougher chalazae, so it's a good idea to strain the beaten eggs through a sieve.

5 Seasoning eggs is almost as personal as eating them. I season my eggs after cooking because I like the taste and texture of the seasonings on top of the eggs, but if you wish, beat the seasonings into the beaten eggs. Salt does not make the eggs tough, as some cooks assert.

6 It's always best to serve eggs immediately and, if possible, on warmed plates. If absolutely necessary, though, you can keep the eggs warm in a 170°F oven while you make more batches. But never hold cooked eggs for longer than 5 minutes, or they will lose their delicate texture.

7 If you are making a few omelets at a time, create a production line using two skillets. Then turn the cooked omelets out onto their plates and keep warm in the oven while you make more.

Soft- or Hard-Boiled Eggs

PLACE THE EGGS IN A SAUCEPAN AND ADD ENOUGH COLD WATER TO COVER THEM BY 1 INCH. BRING JUST TO A BOIL OVER HIGH HEAT, REMOVE FROM THE HEAT, AND COVER. *For soft-boiled eggs,* let stand for 4 minutes. *For hard-boiled eggs,* let stand for 15 minutes. (Do not let the eggs stand for longer than 15 minutes, or they will overcook and develop green rings around the yolks.) When the eggs are ready, drain them and run cold water over them to stop the cooking. Hard-boiled eggs are easiest to peel when still warm. If you have to peel chilled eggs, run hot water over them for a minute or so to warm them slightly.

Deviled Egg Salad

Makes about 3¼ cups; 10 to 12 servings

I'm an egg salad purist. The dill and chives add a bright herbaceous bite to this egg salad, but I enjoy it just as much without them. The creamy mayonnaise tempers the sharp heat of mustard in this classic deviled egg combination.

½ cup (116 grams) mayonnaise

½ cup (70 grams) finely diced celery heart (strings removed with a vegetable peeler before chopping)

1 tablespoon coarsely chopped fresh dill

2 teaspoons finely chopped fresh chives

1 teaspoon dry mustard powder, preferably Colman's

¼ teaspoon sweet Hungarian paprika

10 large hard-boiled eggs (page 189), peeled and cut into ¼-inch dice

Fine sea salt and freshly ground black pepper

1 In a large bowl, stir together the mayonnaise, celery, dill, chives, mustard, and paprika.

2 Add the eggs and fold gently until well mixed. Season to taste with salt and pepper. Serve immediately, or cover and refrigerate for up to overnight.

Egg Salad Biscuits: Make a double batch of Water Mill Biscuits (page 118), for 20 to 24 biscuits total. Split the biscuits and spread a spoonful of egg salad on each bottom half. Top with tender greens, such as pea shoots, and sandwich with the tops of the biscuits (photo opposite).

Poached Eggs

At home and at our restaurants, we always use egg poachers because that's the easiest way to perfectly poach eggs, whether we're doing two or twelve. My home poacher is the best egg poacher on the planet. It's made by Endurance and has a 6-cup tray that holds the egg cups nicely above the simmering water. A central handle allows you to lift the eggs out all at once. Best of all, it has a little hole in the glass top so the steam can escape, reducing the amount of water dripping onto your beautiful eggs.

To poach eggs in an egg poacher, simply bring 1½ inches of water to a full boil in a deep skillet over high heat, then reduce the heat to low to keep the water at a simmer. Brush the insides of the poaching cups with Clarified Butter (page 54) and immediately crack an egg into each. Poach according to the manufacturer's directions until the whites are set, about 3 minutes. Remove the eggs and let drain on paper towels, if needed. Serve hot.

If you don't want to use a poacher, bring 1½ inches of water to a full boil in a deep skillet over high heat, then reduce the heat to low to keep the water at a simmer. Crack each egg into a ramekin. Gently slide the eggs, one at a time, into the simmering water. Simmer, spooning the white of each egg back over on itself to help the egg keep an oval shape, until the whites are set, about 3 minutes. Using a slotted spoon, lift out each egg and drain on paper towels.

Classic Eggs Benedict

Makes 6 servings

Believe it or not, I didn't have eggs Benedict on the menu when I first opened Sarabeth's. Since we started serving them, we've turned out countless orders. Our customers in Japan are especially big fans. I stick to classic hollandaise and take my time with it—especially when adding the softened butter—so that it doesn't break. The silken sauce, rich yet light from continuous whisking, cloaks the eggs and my signature English muffins.

Hollandaise

3 large egg yolks, at room temperature
1 tablespoon water
8 ounces (227 grams) unsalted butter, softened
1 tablespoon plus 1 teaspoon fresh lemon juice
Fine sea salt

12 thin slices best-quality ham, warmed
12 Poached Eggs (page 192), hot
6 Whole Wheat English Muffins (page 147), tops trimmed flat, split into halves, and toasted
Finely diced red and yellow bell peppers, for garnish
Snipped fresh chives, for garnish
Freshly ground black pepper, for garnish

1 To prepare the hollandaise: Fill the bottom of a double boiler or a large saucepan halfway with water and bring to a simmer. In the top of the double boiler or a nonreactive metal bowl that fits snugly over the saucepan, whisk the egg yolks and water.

2 Set the top of the double boiler or bowl over the simmering water and whisk until the yolks are very pale and thick, about 3 minutes. If the mixture begins to heat too quickly and threatens to curdle and get lumpy, remove the top pan or bowl from the saucepan and whisk for a while before setting it over the simmering water again. When the yolks are ready, you should be able to see the bottom of the bowl with each stroke.

3 Continue to whisk while adding the butter a little at a time. When all of the butter has been incorporated and the mixture is silky smooth, whisk in the lemon juice and season to taste with salt.

4 Place 1 warm ham slice and then 1 hot poached egg, yolk side down, on top of each freshly toasted English muffin half. Spoon the hollandaise sauce on top, letting it run down the sides of the eggs and muffins. Garnish with the bell peppers, chives, and black pepper. Serve immediately.

Eggs Benedict with Gravlax: Substitute thin slices of Three-Herb Gravlax (page 254) for the ham.

Fried Eggs

In a skillet, heat a thin coating of clarified butter (page 54) over medium heat. Crack the egg or eggs into the skillet, reduce the heat to low, and cook to the desired doneness. For sunny-side-up eggs, cover the skillet and cook until the whites are set. For over-easy, once the whites are set, carefully turn the eggs to cook the other side. If you wish, spoon some of the butter over the eggs to speed up the cooking process, but keep the heat low. High heat makes tough eggs.

Ultimate Scrambled Eggs

Makes 1 serving

Perfect scrambled eggs are golden and soft, almost fluffy. The key is gentle handling. Fold the eggs over on themselves in the skillet to retain as much air as possible. I don't cook them over high heat—low heat keeps the eggs creamy. For more servings, you can increase the amount of eggs and pan size as needed, up to 12 eggs in a 12-inch skillet. Add only 1 more teaspoon clarified butter for every 3 additional eggs.

3 large eggs

2 teaspoons Clarified Butter (page 54)

Fine sea salt and freshly ground black pepper

1 In a medium bowl, using an immersion (stick) blender or wire whisk, beat the eggs until completely combined.

2 In a nonstick medium skillet, heat the clarified butter over medium heat just until very hot. Add the eggs, immediately reduce the heat to low, and cook just until the eggs are set around the edges. Using a silicone spatula, fold the eggs over on themselves. Cook until the edges set again and repeat the folding, continuing until the eggs are set into soft, moist curds (or longer, if you prefer). Immediately transfer to a warm plate. Keep in mind that the eggs will continue to cook and firm up a bit outside of the skillet. The entire procedure should take no more than 2 minutes. Season with salt and pepper and serve immediately.

Popeye Eggs with Country Ham: Divide 1 cup (48 grams) baby spinach, stems removed, wilted, between a split, toasted, and buttered Whole Wheat English Muffin (page 147). Top with 1 ounce (28 grams) warm, thinly sliced country ham and the scrambled eggs.

Green-and-White Scrambled Eggs: Heat the clarified butter in the skillet. Add the finely chopped green part of 1 scallion and cook until wilted, about 30 seconds. Add the eggs and cook as directed above until almost done but still quite moist. Add 1½ ounces (44 grams) cream cheese, cut into ¼- to ½-inch cubes. Remove the pan from the heat and fold in the cream cheese. (It is very important not to add the cream cheese too soon, or it will melt and disappear.) Let the eggs stand, off the heat, to finish cooking in the retained heat of the pan. Season with salt and pepper. Serve with Popovers (page 150), if desired (photo page 196).

Goldie Lox: Follow the instructions for Green-and-White Scrambled Eggs, omitting the scallion. Add 1½ ounces (44 grams) Scottish or Irish smoked salmon, sliced into thin strips, along with the cream cheese cubes, and proceed as directed above.

Fluffy Scrambled Eggs

Makes 1 serving

Adding cream to the beaten eggs creates even airier scrambled eggs. And to complement that milky taste, I use regular butter, which has more flavor than clarified. The final seasoning comes only at the end. I don't salt the eggs while they're cooking because that compromises the texture of the egg-cream mixture.

2 large eggs
¼ cup (58 grams) heavy cream
1 teaspoon unsalted butter
Fine sea salt and freshly ground black pepper

1 In a medium bowl, whisk the eggs until frothy. Add the cream and continue whisking until very pale yellow.

2 Heat a nonstick medium skillet over medium heat until the surface is warm. Reduce the heat to low and add the butter. When the butter melts and bubbles, add the egg mixture and cook just until set around the edges. Using a silicone spatula, push the edges in toward the center of the pan to create florets in the egg mixture. Cook until the edges set again, then repeat, continuing until the eggs are set into soft, moist curds (or longer, if you prefer). Immediately transfer to a warm plate. Keep in mind that the eggs will continue to cook and firm up a bit outside of the skillet. The entire procedure should take no more than 2 minutes.

3 Season with salt and pepper and serve immediately.

Scrambled Eggs with Garlic Croutons: Stir ⅓ cup homemade or bakery-bought garlic croutons into the beaten egg-cream mixture before cooking (photo page 198).

The Perfect Omelet

Makes 1 serving

There is an art to making an omelet. What you're looking for is a velvety smooth, tender omelet without hills, valleys, or wrinkles, with a light-as-a-cloud texture and a pale yellow exterior unmarred by brown spots (caused by high heat). Do not be discouraged if your first attempts don't match that description. Practice makes perfect when it comes to my technique. It's worth the effort to keep working at it until you get it right. Whether you serve your omelet plain or filled, it should be plump and moist.

3 large eggs

2 teaspoons Clarified Butter (page 54)

Fine sea salt and freshly ground black pepper

1 In a medium bowl, using an immersion (stick) blender or whisk, beat the eggs until completely combined. Strain the eggs into another bowl to remove any thick strands of chalazae.

2 In a nonstick medium skillet, heat the clarified butter over medium-high heat until hot. Add the eggs, but do not stir until a bubble appears in the center of the pan. Using a silicone spatula, stir the eggs with a quick circular motion for 10 seconds, then reduce the heat to medium, wait for the bubble to appear again, and stir for another 10 seconds. Reduce the heat to medium-low and continue to cook until the eggs on top are slightly runny. Using the spatula, gently pull the edges of the omelet away from the pan.

3 Give the pan a little shake to free the omelet from the bottom, then flip the omelet over to the other side with a gentle upward motion of your wrist. Cook for 15 seconds. Flip the omelet again and slide it halfway out of the pan onto a warm plate. Fold the rest of the omelet over onto the plate, gently shaping it into a half-moon. Season with salt and pepper and serve immediately.

Gruyère, Nut, and Honey Omelet: In a small dry skillet, cook 2 to 3 tablespoons pine nuts or unsalted hulled sunflower seeds over medium heat, stirring occasionally, until toasted, about 3 minutes. Transfer to a plate and cool. Add half of the nuts to the beaten eggs and cook as directed above. Slide the omelet halfway out of the pan onto a warm plate. Sprinkle ⅓ cup (about 1½ ounces; 44 grams) shredded Gruyère cheese onto that part of the omelet, then fold the rest of the omelet over onto the plate, gently shaping it into a half-moon. Season with salt and pepper. Drizzle 1 teaspoon full-flavored honey (acacia or chestnut honey is wonderful) over the omelet and sprinkle with the remaining nuts.

Sweet Jam and Cream Cheese Omelet: Make the omelet as directed (page 199), but omit the salt and pepper. Slide the omelet halfway out of the pan onto a warm plate. Place 2 tablespoons Fig Jam (page 180; or use store-bought) and 1½ ounces (44 grams) cream cheese, cut into ½-inch cubes, on that part of the omelet. Fold the rest of the omelet over onto the plate, gently shaping it into a half-moon.

Cheddar and Apple Butter Omelet: Make the omelet as directed (page 199), but omit the salt and pepper. Slide the omelet halfway out of the pan onto a warm plate. Place ⅓ cup (about 1½ ounces; 44 grams) shredded sharp Cheddar cheese and 2 tablespoons Chunky Apple Butter (page 181; or use store-bought Sarabeth's Chunky Apple Preserves) on that part of the omelet. Fold the rest of the omelet over onto the plate, gently shaping it into a half-moon.

Spinach and Goat Cheese Egg White Omelet: Substitute 4 large egg whites for the eggs. Form 1 ounce (28 grams) fresh goat cheese into a 3-inch-long cylinder and set aside. Heat the clarified butter in the skillet. Add ½ cup (28 grams) packed baby spinach to the pan and cook until wilted. Add the egg whites and cook as directed (page 199) until completely set. Slide the omelet halfway out of the pan onto a warm plate. Place the goat cheese on that part of the omelet and fold the rest of the omelet over onto the plate, gently shaping it into a half-moon. Season with salt and pepper (photo opposite).

The Red Omelet

Makes 4 servings

This sauce-smothered cheesy omelet is a thing of beauty—and the tomato sauce is one of the best. A combination of four different kinds of onion and a touch of butter, in addition to olive oil, takes it out of the ordinary. The sauce makes enough for four omelets. Set yourself up with two nonstick skillets so you can make the omelets quickly, in an orderly fashion, and serve them as soon as possible.

Red Sauce

2 tablespoons Clarified Butter (page 54)

1 medium red bell pepper (5 ounces; 142 grams), cored, seeded, and cut into 1/8-inch-wide strips (see Cook's Note on page 241)

1 small onion (3 ounces; 85 grams), finely chopped

1 scallion, finely chopped

1½ tablespoons finely chopped shallots

1 medium garlic clove, minced

1 cup (240 grams) canned diced tomatoes in thick puree

⅓ cup (75 grams) water

1 tablespoon extra-virgin olive oil

2 teaspoons finely chopped fresh oregano

1 teaspoon granulated sugar

Fine sea salt and freshly ground black pepper

12 large eggs

8 teaspoons Clarified Butter (page 54)

4 ounces (114 grams) Monterey Jack or extra-sharp Cheddar cheese, shredded (1 cup)

½ cup (121 grams) sour cream

Chopped fresh chives, for garnish

1 To make the red sauce: In a medium saucepan, heat the clarified butter over medium heat. Add the bell pepper and onion and cook, stirring often, until softened, about 5 minutes. Add the scallion, shallots, and garlic and cook until the shallots are tender, about 2 minutes. Stir in the tomatoes, water, oil, oregano, and sugar and season with salt and pepper. Bring to a simmer, then reduce the heat to low and simmer until slightly thickened, about 15 minutes. Keep warm over low heat. (The sauce can be cooled to room temperature, covered, and refrigerated for up to 2 days. Reheat before using.)

2 Position a rack in the center of the oven and preheat to 200°F.

3 In a medium bowl, using an immersion (stick) blender or whisk, beat the eggs until completely combined. Strain the eggs into another bowl to remove any thick strands of chalazae.

4 In a nonstick medium skillet, heat 2 teaspoons clarified butter over medium-high heat until hot. If you have two nonstick skillets, make 2 omelets at a time. Add ¾ cup eggs, but do not stir until a bubble appears in the center of the pan. Using a silicone spatula, stir the eggs with a quick circular motion for 10 seconds, then reduce the heat to medium, wait for the bubble to appear again, and stir for another 10 seconds. Reduce the heat to medium-low and continue to cook until the eggs on top are slightly runny. Using the spatula, gently pull the edges of the omelet away from the pan.

5 Give the pan a little shake to free the omelet from the bottom, then flip the omelet over to the other side with a gentle upward motion of your wrist. Cook for 15 seconds. Flip the omelet again and slide it halfway out of the pan onto a warm plate. Place ¼ cup cheese on that part of the omelet. Fold the rest of the omelet over onto the plate, gently shaping it into a half-moon. Season with salt and pepper. Keep warm in the oven while you use the remaining clarified butter, eggs, and cheese to make 3 more omelets.

6 To serve, cut a 2-inch-long slit in the center of each omelet. Spread each slit open to make a pocket and spoon 2 tablespoons sour cream into the pocket. Then top the omelets with the red sauce. Sprinkle with chives and serve immediately.

Farmer's Omelet
with Leeks, Speck, and Potato

Makes 1 serving

Speck, a type of Italian ham similar to prosciutto, has a smoky saltiness that does wonders for eggs. Not only does it lend its irresistible savory meaty flavor to this fluffy omelet, it also stays crisp. With each bite, you get soft caramelized leeks, tender golden potato slices, and crunchy cured pork. The trio makes the omelet taste hearty but not the least bit heavy.

1 teaspoon extra-virgin olive oil

3 teaspoons Clarified Butter (page 54)

1 small leek (4 ounces; 114 grams), white and pale green parts only, washed well and very thinly sliced (¼ cup)

Freshly ground black pepper

½ small Yukon Gold potato, scrubbed, cut lengthwise in half, and very thinly sliced (¼ cup)

1 ounce (28 grams) speck, finely diced (¼ cup)

3 large eggs

Fine sea salt

1 In a nonstick small skillet, heat the oil and 1 teaspoon clarified butter over medium-high heat. Add the leek, season with pepper, and cook, stirring, until fragrant, about 1 minute. Add the potato and cook, stirring occasionally, until almost tender, about 4 minutes. Add the speck and cook, stirring occasionally, until lightly browned, about 5 minutes. Remove from the heat and set aside.

2 In a medium bowl, using an immersion (stick) blender or whisk, beat the eggs until completely combined. Strain the eggs into another bowl to remove any thick strands of chalazae.

3 In a nonstick medium skillet, heat the remaining 2 teaspoons clarified butter over medium-high heat until hot. Add the eggs, but do not stir until a bubble appears in the center of the pan. Using a silicone spatula, stir the eggs with a quick circular motion for 10 seconds, then reduce the heat to medium, wait for the bubble to appear again, and stir for another 10 seconds. Reduce the heat to medium-low and continue to cook until the eggs on top are slightly runny. Using the spatula, gently pull the edges of the omelet away from the pan.

4 Give the pan a little shake to free the omelet from the bottom, then flip the omelet over to the other side with a gentle upward motion of your wrist. Cook for 15 seconds. Flip the omelet again and slide it halfway out of the pan onto a warm plate. Sprinkle the potato mixture over that part of the omelet. Fold the rest of the omelet over onto the plate, gently shaping it into a half-moon. Season with salt and pepper and serve immediately.

Chapter Nine

Frittatas and Stratas

When you want to serve eggs to a crowd without being tied to the stove, baked eggs are the way to go. They may take longer to cook than stovetop eggs, but that time is quite short and largely unattended. All you need to do is time it so that you pull the dish out of the oven right before you want to eat. This strategy also makes these hearty dishes ideal for dinner.

Baked eggs fall into two categories. Both frittatas and stratas contain fillings that bake with the eggs, but stratas also incorporate bread. Frittatas taste just as satisfying without bread, as the mix-ins are evenly dispersed throughout the eggs during baking. Frittatas develop their signature shape and omelet-meets-custard texture with a two-step process: They are started on the stovetop, cooked almost like scrambled eggs to set the eggs and make them fluffy, and then finished in the oven, to puff them and melt any cheeses on top. For stratas, an egg custard soaks into the bread before baking. While you can soak the bread for just an hour, a night in the refrigerator makes a world of difference. Then all of the filling flavors meld together as the bread softens into a silky custard when baked.

KEY INGREDIENT

Half-and-Half: For stratas, eggs are mixed into a custard with milk and cream for soaking the bread. I use half-and-half to cut those two ingredients down to one. If you have any left over, warm it to serve with hot coffee.

TOOL KIT

Ovenproof Nonstick Skillet: Frittatas are started on the stovetop, then finished in the oven. Be sure to use a nonstick skillet that can withstand the heat of the oven; check the manufacturer's specifications for the handle.

Baking Dishes: You'll need a range of different sizes of baking dishes for stratas, from individual 6-ounce ramekins to 3-quart casseroles. Any ovenproof glass or ceramic dish will do, but I love preparing these in dishes attractive enough for the table.

Margherita Frittata
with Tomato, Mozzarella, and Basil

Makes 2 servings

Three simple Italian ingredients—tomato, mozzarella, and basil—work magic in every form. When nestled into eggs, they make a delicious dish that would be welcome at breakfast, lunch, or dinner. Be sure to use the best mozzarella here. If you can find smoked mozzarella, you might want to give it a try. It adds a complex depth of flavor.

4 large eggs

2 teaspoons Clarified Butter (page 54)

1 large plum tomato, cored, seeded, and cut into ¼-inch dice (½ cup)

Kosher salt and freshly ground black pepper

2 ounces (57 grams) fresh mozzarella, preferably smoked, coarsely grated

1 tablespoon packed fresh basil leaves, very thinly sliced

1 Position a rack in the center of the oven and preheat to 350°F.

2 In a medium bowl, using an immersion (stick) blender or whisk, beat the eggs until well combined. Strain the eggs through a fine-mesh sieve into another bowl to remove any thick strands of chalazae.

3 In an ovenproof nonstick 8½-inch skillet, heat the clarified butter over medium heat. Add the tomato, season with salt and pepper, and cook, tossing, for 1 minute. Add the eggs and immediately reduce the heat to medium-low. Cook the eggs just until they are set around the edges. Using a silicone spatula, stir the eggs 2 or 3 revolutions, just to combine the cooked and uncooked portions. Continue cooking until the eggs are set around the edges again, then lift up the edges of the frittata with the spatula and tilt the pan to allow any uncooked eggs to flow underneath the frittata. Cook until the edges set once again and repeat the tilting procedure. The frittata should look shiny and uncooked on top. Sprinkle the cheese and basil on top.

4 Place in the oven and bake until the cheese is melted and the frittata is slightly puffed, about 5 minutes. Cut into wedges and serve.

Goat Cheese and Gruyère Frittata
with Arugula Salad

Makes 6 servings

What's really nice here is the way the two cheeses play off each other. The sharp, tangy goat cheese gets very soft and the stronger Gruyère becomes melty, but each maintains its own identity. Peppery arugula ties it all together. The cooked greens wilt into the cheesy frittata, and the bright arugula side salad cuts through the richness of the frittata and makes this a complete meal.

12 large eggs

2 tablespoons Clarified Butter (page 54) or extra-virgin olive oil

1 cup (28 grams) packed arugula

3 ounces (85 grams) Gruyère cheese, coarsely grated (⅔ cup)

3 ounces (85 grams) fresh goat cheese, broken into small pieces

Salad

2 cups (58 grams) packed arugula

Juice of ½ small lemon

2 tablespoons extra-virgin olive oil

Kosher salt and freshly ground black pepper

⅓ cup (50 grams) raw hulled sunflower seeds, toasted (page 41)

1 Position a rack in the center of the oven and preheat to 350°F. (This is a good time to toast the sunflower seeds for the salad.)

2 In a large bowl, using an immersion (stick) blender or whisk, beat the eggs until well combined. Strain the eggs through a fine-mesh sieve into another bowl to remove any thick strands of chalazae.

3 In an ovenproof nonstick 10-inch skillet, heat 1 tablespoon clarified butter over medium heat. Add the arugula and cook, stirring, for 1 minute. Add the remaining 1 tablespoon clarified butter and the eggs and immediately reduce the heat to medium-low. Cook the eggs just until they are set around the edges. Using a silicone spatula, stir the eggs 2 or 3 revolutions, just to combine the cooked and uncooked portions. Continue cooking until the eggs are set around the edges again, then lift up the edges of the frittata with the spatula and tilt the pan to allow any uncooked eggs to flow underneath the frittata. Add the Gruyère and goat cheese and cook until the edges set once again, then repeat the tilting procedure. The frittata should look shiny and uncooked on top; the cheeses will not be melted yet.

4 Place in the oven and bake until the cheeses are melted and the frittata is slightly puffed, about 8 minutes.

5 While the frittata bakes, prepare the salad: In a large bowl, toss the arugula with the lemon juice and oil. Season to taste with salt and pepper and toss again.

6 To serve, cut the frittata into wedges and top with the arugula salad. Sprinkle each serving with some of the toasted sunflower seeds.

Shrimp and Tarragon Frittata

Makes 6 servings

Shellfish may not be the first thing that comes to mind when considering breakfast, but shrimp is a great way to start the day. It goes especially well with eggs and feels like a luxurious treat. When I want to make this dish even more special, I bake it in a cake ring to make the frittata taller. After the egg mixture cooks in the skillet on the stove, I slide it into a buttered tall 6-inch-diameter cake ring set on a parchment paper–lined half-sheet pan, pressing the mixture gently into the ring to make it an even layer. Then I transfer it to the oven and bake. When it comes out, I run a thin knife around the edges and lift off the ring. The elegant tower makes a stunning brunch dish.

10 large eggs

2 tablespoons Clarified Butter (page 54)

8 ounces (227 grams) jumbo (16–20 count) shrimp, peeled, deveined, and cut into ½-inch pieces

Kosher salt and freshly ground black pepper

1 medium garlic clove, finely chopped

1 teaspoon packed fresh tarragon leaves, finely chopped, plus extra leaves for garnish

1 teaspoon fresh lemon juice

1 Position a rack in the center of the oven and preheat to 350°F.

2 In a large bowl, using an immersion (stick) blender or whisk, beat the eggs until well combined. Strain the eggs through a fine-mesh sieve into another bowl to remove any thick strands of chalazae.

3 In an ovenproof nonstick 12-inch skillet, heat 1 tablespoon clarified butter over medium-high heat. Add the shrimp, season with salt and pepper, and cook, stirring and tossing, until just opaque, about 2 minutes. Add the garlic and cook, stirring, until just golden, about 30 seconds. Stir in the tarragon and lemon juice.

4 Add the remaining 1 tablespoon clarified butter and the eggs and immediately reduce the heat to medium-low. Season the eggs with a pinch of salt. Cook the eggs just until they are set around the edges. Using a silicone spatula, stir the eggs 2 or 3 revolutions, just to combine the cooked and uncooked portions. Continue cooking until the eggs are set around the edges again, then lift up the edges of the frittata with the spatula and tilt the pan to allow any uncooked eggs to flow underneath the frittata. Cook until the edges set once again and repeat the tilting procedure. The frittata should look shiny and uncooked on top.

5 Place in the oven and bake until the frittata is slightly puffed, about 10 minutes. Garnish with tarragon leaves, cut into wedges, and serve.

Vegetable Ricotta Frittata

Makes 4 servings

A well-made frittata reminds me of an "egg pizza." While I love the plump perfection of an individual omelet, I like that the frittata has the advantage of serving more people. This vegetarian frittata is light and delicious, but it can be made more substantial with a side of grilled Italian sausages. Although ricotta is a milder cheese than one might expect in a frittata, it melts into a smooth creaminess that is very pleasant.

2 tablespoons unsalted butter
¼ cup finely chopped red bell pepper
2 tablespoons chopped shallots
1 cup (232 grams) shredded zucchini
Kosher salt and freshly ground black pepper
2 teaspoons fresh oregano leaves, finely chopped
6 large eggs
2 teaspoons Clarified Butter (page 54)
6 tablespoons (85 grams) fresh whole-milk ricotta cheese

1 In a medium skillet, melt the unsalted butter over medium heat. Add the bell pepper and shallots and cook, stirring, just until barely softened, about 1 minute. Add the zucchini, season with salt and pepper, and cook until softened, about 3 minutes. Stir in the oregano. Set aside to cool to lukewarm.

2 Position a rack in the center of the oven and preheat to 350°F.

3 In a large bowl, using an immersion (stick) blender or whisk, beat the eggs until well combined. Strain the eggs through a fine-mesh sieve into another bowl to remove any thick strands of chalazae. Stir in the vegetables.

4 In an ovenproof nonstick 10-inch skillet, heat the clarified butter over medium heat. Add the egg mixture and immediately reduce the heat to medium-low. Cook the eggs just until they are set around the edges. Using a silicone spatula, stir the eggs 2 or 3 revolutions, just to combine the cooked and uncooked portions. Continue cooking until the eggs are set around the edges again, then lift up the edges of the frittata with the spatula and tilt the pan to allow any uncooked eggs to flow underneath the frittata. Cook until the edges set once again, and repeat the tilting procedure. The frittata should look shiny and uncooked on top. Sprinkle the ricotta on top.

5 Place in the oven and bake until the frittata is slightly puffed, about 10 minutes. Cut into wedges and serve.

Individual Croissant Vegetable Stratas

Makes 6 servings

Sometimes a dish starts with an actual dish. I spotted some gorgeous gray Staub mini cocottes at a sale and just had to have them. I bought half a dozen and immediately knew I wanted to use them for these stratas. Because of the croissants' rounded shape, two cross-cut slices fit snugly in my individual round casseroles. And because croissants are rich, I layered them with vegetables—cauliflower and mushrooms—which taste light and take well to butter.

COOK'S NOTE: The stratas need to be assembled ahead and refrigerated overnight before baking.

Softened unsalted butter, for the dishes

1 tablespoon plus 5 teaspoons Clarified Butter (page 54)

½ small Vidalia onion, very thinly sliced

Kosher salt and freshly ground black pepper

1 large garlic clove, minced

8 ounces (227 grams) cauliflower, trimmed and broken into ½-inch florets

4 ounces (114 grams) cremini mushrooms, stems removed and caps thinly sliced

5 large eggs

2 cups (456 grams) half-and-half

⅛ teaspoon freshly grated nutmeg

3 best-quality croissants, cut crosswise into twenty-four ½-inch slices

4 ounces (114 grams) Gruyère cheese, coarsely grated (scant 1 cup)

1 tablespoon finely chopped fresh flat-leaf parsley leaves

1 Generously butter six 8-ounce cocottes or ramekins. Place on a half-sheet pan.

2 In a 12-inch skillet, heat 1 tablespoon clarified butter over medium-low heat. Add the onion, season with salt and pepper, and cook, stirring occasionally, until just tender, about 5 minutes. Add the garlic and cook, stirring, until just golden, about 30 seconds. Transfer to a large bowl.

3 Wipe out the skillet and heat 4 teaspoons clarified butter over medium heat. Add the cauliflower, season with salt and pepper, and cook, stirring and tossing occasionally, until browned, about 10 minutes. Transfer to the bowl with the onion mixture.

STAUB
STAUB

4 Wipe out the skillet and heat the remaining 1 teaspoon clarified butter over medium heat. Add the mushrooms, season with salt and pepper, and cook, stirring occasionally, until lightly browned, about 5 minutes. Transfer to the bowl with the other vegetables.

5 In another large bowl, using an immersion (stick) blender or whisk, beat the eggs with the half-and-half, nutmeg, and a pinch each of salt and pepper until completely combined.

6 Fit 2 croissant slices snugly into the bottom of each cocotte to make an even layer. Divide half of the vegetable filling, Gruyère, and parsley among the cocottes, spreading them evenly. Pour half of the egg mixture into the cocottes. Repeat the layering once with the remaining croissants, filling, Gruyère, parsley, and egg mixture. Cover the stratas tightly with plastic wrap and refrigerate overnight.

7 When ready to bake, let the stratas stand at room temperature for 1 hour and then uncover them. Position a rack in the center of the oven and preheat to 325°F.

8 If using cocottes, cover the stratas with the lids. If using ramekins, cover with parchment-lined foil (or, a piece of parchment paper, then aluminum foil). Bake for 15 minutes, then uncover and bake until the tops are golden and the stratas are cooked through, about 15 minutes longer. Serve hot or warm.

Two-Cheese Strata
with Broccoli Rabe and Sausage

Makes 12 servings

Each forkful of this decadent dish, layered like lasagna, gives you a hit of all the ingredients. The bite of broccoli rabe cuts through the richness of the browned sausage, melty Fontina cheese, and salty Pecorino Romano. Because the strata, made with tender white bread, is assembled ahead so it soaks in the egg custard overnight, the flavors fuse together when baked.

COOK'S NOTE: The strata needs to be assembled and refrigerated overnight before baking.

Softened unsalted butter, for the baking dish

2 tablespoons extra-virgin olive oil

12 ounces (340 grams) broccoli rabe, trimmed and cut into 1-inch pieces

Kosher salt and freshly ground black pepper

½ teaspoon fresh lemon juice

9 ounces (255 grams) sweet Italian sausage, cut into ½-inch pieces

10 large eggs

4 cups (912 grams) half-and-half

1 loaf (1 pound; 454 grams) sliced best-quality pain de mie or other tender white bread, preferably day-old, crusts trimmed

6 ounces (170 grams) Fontina cheese, coarsely grated (1⅓ cups)

2 tablespoons finely grated Pecorino Romano cheese

1 Generously butter a 13 by 9 by 2-inch glass or ceramic baking dish.

2 In a medium skillet, heat 1 tablespoon oil over medium heat. Add the broccoli rabe, season with salt and pepper, and cook, stirring occasionally, until bright green and crisp-tender, about 5 minutes. Stir in the lemon juice, then transfer to a medium bowl.

3 Wipe out the skillet and heat the remaining 1 tablespoon oil over medium heat. Add the sausage and cook, turning occasionally, until evenly browned and cooked through, about 8 minutes. Remove from the heat.

4 In a large bowl, using an immersion (stick) blender or whisk, beat the eggs with the half-and-half and a pinch each of salt and pepper until completely combined.

5 Arrange half of the bread slices in the bottom of the buttered dish in a single layer with no gaps, cutting slices to fit as needed. Spread half of the broccoli rabe, sausage, and Fontina evenly on top, then pour over half of the egg mixture. Repeat the layering once with the remaining bread, broccoli rabe, sausage, Fontina, and egg mixture. Sprinkle the Pecorino Romano evenly on top. Cover tightly with plastic wrap and refrigerate overnight.

6 When ready to bake, let the strata stand at room temperature for 1 hour, then uncover. Position a rack in the center of the oven and preheat to 350°F.

7 Bake until the top is browned and the strata is cooked through, about 1 hour. Cut into squares to serve hot or warm.

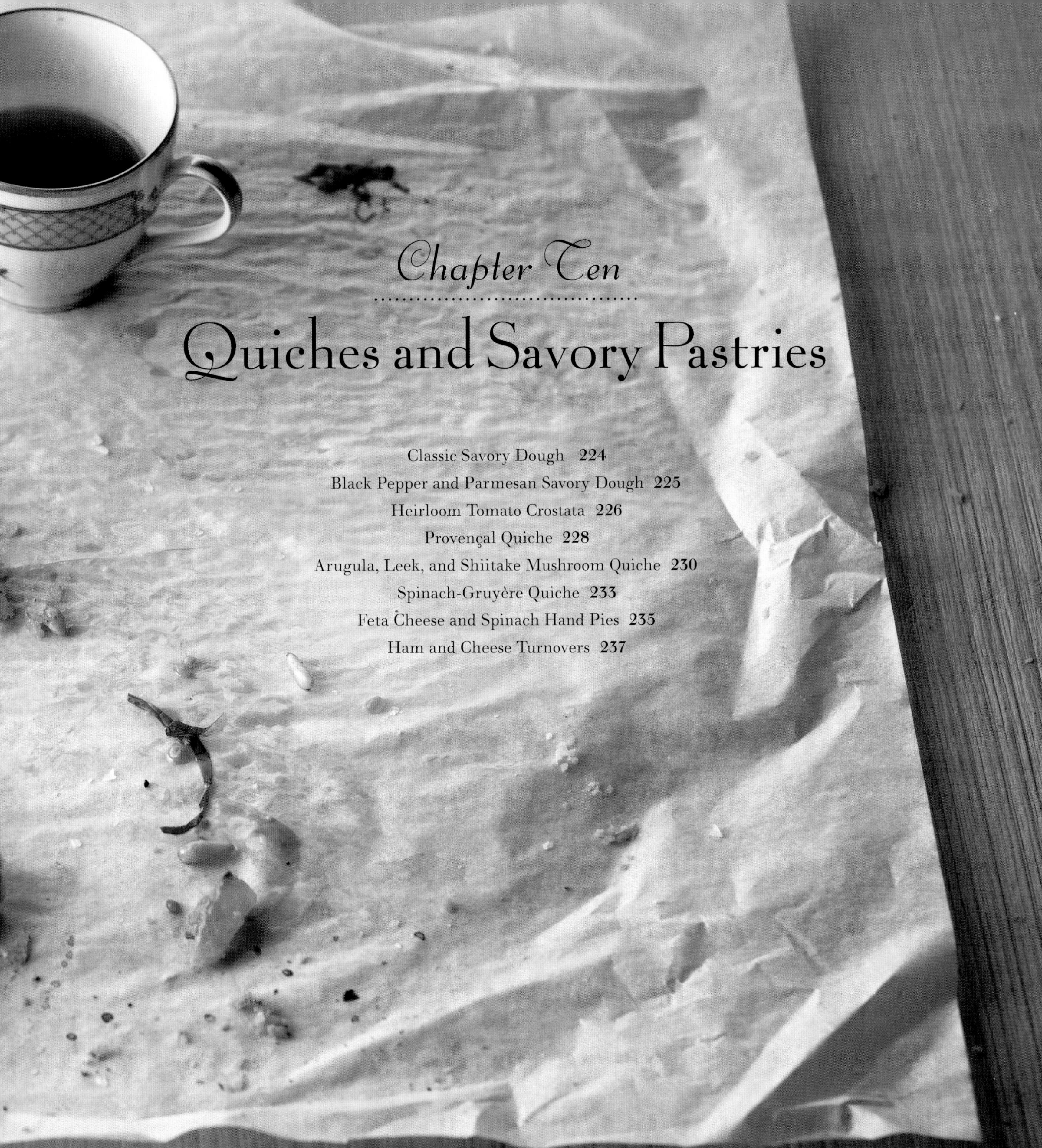

Chapter Ten

Quiches and Savory Pastries

I JUST LOVE DAIRY—ANYTHING WITH HEAVY CREAM, THE SMELL OF BUTTER, CHEESE IN ALL FORMS. WHAT I LIKE ABOUT QUICHES IS THAT THEY DELIVER the best of two worlds: the baking world and the cheesy world. When you eat a great quiche, you get the right balance of cream and cheese and light pastry. A slice of quiche is right up there with other great transcendent meals I have enjoyed. I like quiche best an hour after it's come out of the oven, when it's neither cold nor scalding hot. That still-warm temperature is when you can taste the flavors the most.

For savory pastries, I rely on two crusts: One is a tender, buttery savory dough that tastes wonderful with a variety of fillings. The other includes Parmesan cheese, black pepper, and oyster crackers. With its crunchy texture and pronounced saltiness, this dough works well with mixtures that are mild enough not to overpower it but still assertive enough to stand up to it. Both doughs come together easily in a stand mixer, which requires the quantities for a double batch to mix them properly. That's not a problem, though—it's handy to have the dough for two crusts on hand when you're cooking for a crowd, and if you're not, the extra dough freezes well. With my irresistible filling options, you'll want to try all of the creative yet comforting combinations of eggs, cheese, and vegetables.

TOOL KIT

Pie and Tart Pans: For pie dishes, use a 9-inch glass pan (not deep-dish), which allows you to see when the pastry has browned and crisped on the bottom. For tart pans, make sure the bottoms are removable and the sides are 1¼ inches tall. A dark surface helps crisp the entire crust, preventing a wet bottom, so the tart will stand firm after unmolding. For free-form tarts, use a half-sheet pan lined with parchment paper.

TIPS FOR PERFECT CRUST

1 Don't overhandle the dough, or the crust will be tough. When adding the flour to the butter mixture, mix just until the ingredients are combined and clump together.

2 Chill the dough disks to firm up the butter and allow the gluten to relax. Two hours is optimum, because the dough will be chilled through but still supple enough to roll out easily. If the dough is too cold, it will crack during rolling. In that case, let the dough stand at room temperature for 20 to 30 minutes to soften slightly and reduce the chill. (If it still cracks, you can always piece it back together.)

3 Prep the dough for rolling by tapping the entire circumference of the disk against the work surface and then gently tapping the top of the dough with the rolling pin to soften it a little. These steps will prevent cracking and make rolling easier.

4 To create a perfect round, start from the center and roll away from yourself. Then rotate the dough 90 degrees and roll again. Keep rotating and rolling, flouring as needed to prevent sticking, until the dough circle is 9 inches in diameter. Then finish rolling to your desired thickness and size without rotating it again.

5 The simplest way to center the dough in the pan is to roll it up onto the rolling pin, then unroll it into the pan. Gently ease the dough into the edges of the pan. For a pie dish, trim the excess dough to a ½- to 1-inch overhang with a sharp knife or kitchen shears. Tuck in the overhang so that the edges of the dough are flush with the rim of the pan. If desired, you can decoratively crimp the edges by pinching the dough all the way around. For a tart pan, be sure to press the dough into the fluted grooves of the pan, letting the dough extend over the edges of the pan. Run the rolling pin over the top of the pan to cut off the excess dough.

6 If the crust is to be prebaked, pierce the dough with a fork in a uniform pattern. Be sure to prick the sides too.

7 Freeze both pie and tart shells until very firm, at least 15 minutes before baking. This helps them hold their shape and not shrink.

8 Put the pie or tart pans on a half-sheet pan before baking to make it easier to get them in and out of the oven. This also helps crisp the bottom crust.

9 Bake in the lower third of the oven to achieve a crisp, brown crust.

10 To partially bake a crust, line the chilled dough with a sheet of parchment paper that extends at least an inch beyond the rim of the pan. Fill with pie weights or dried beans, then bake on the half-sheet pan for 10 minutes. Carefully lift out the paper with the weights. Return the crust to the oven and bake until the surface is golden and dry, about 5 minutes.

Classic Savory Dough

Makes enough for two 9-inch quiches or 8 hand pies or turnovers

For its buttery flavor and crisp texture, a short crust can't be beat. There are important distinctions between pie dough and short crust dough. With an American pie dough, the baker goes for flakiness by cutting cold butter into flour. Here I'm aiming for both crispness and tenderness. To that end, I start by beating the butter to make it airy. Then I add milk, an ingredient you don't find in most pastry doughs. It makes my pastry very forgiving and easy to work with. A touch of sugar also keeps the crust tender. The resulting dough is sturdy enough to hold a wide variety of fillings and delicious enough to eat on its own (so save those scraps and bake them).

1¼ cups (284 grams) unsalted butter, chilled and cut into ½-inch cubes

5 tablespoons (70 grams) whole milk

2¼ cups plus 2 tablespoons (346 grams) unbleached all-purpose flour

2 teaspoons superfine sugar

¼ teaspoon fine sea salt

1 In the bowl of a heavy-duty stand mixer fitted with the paddle attachment, beat the butter on high speed until creamy, about 1 minute. With the machine running, slowly dribble in the milk, occasionally stopping the machine and scraping down the sides of the bowl with a silicone spatula. The mixture should be fluffy, smooth, and shiny, like a buttercream frosting.

2 In a medium bowl, mix the flour, sugar, and salt. With the mixer on low, add the flour mixture and mix just until the dough forms a mass on the paddle and the sides of the bowl are clean.

3 Gather up the dough and transfer to a lightly floured surface. Knead the dough a few times, until it is smooth and supple. Divide it in half and shape into two 6-inch disks. Gently tap the sides of the disks on the work surface all around the circumference (this tamps the dough so the edges won't crack during rolling). Do not overhandle the dough.

4 Wrap the disks in plastic wrap and refrigerate until chilled, about 2 hours. The dough can also be chilled overnight, but it will be very hard and should stand at room temperature for about 30 minutes before rolling out. The wrapped dough can also be frozen in plastic freezer bags for up to 3 weeks. Defrost in the refrigerator overnight before rolling out.

Black Pepper and Parmesan Savory Dough

Makes enough for two 9-inch quiches

To enhance my classic savory dough, I add the crunchy saltiness of oyster crackers and the intensity of Parmesan cheese. This crust packs enough flavor to be eaten as a snack, but it's even more amazing when filled with a cheesy custard.

BAKER'S NOTE: To make oyster cracker crumbs, finely grind oyster crackers in a food processor.

14 tablespoons (198 grams) unsalted butter, chilled and cut into ½-inch cubes

½ cup (112 grams) whole milk

1½ cups (213 grams) unbleached all-purpose flour

1 cup (118 grams) oyster cracker crumbs

1 tablespoon superfine sugar

2 tablespoons finely grated Parmesan cheese

¼ teaspoon freshly ground black pepper

1 In the bowl of a heavy-duty stand mixer fitted with the paddle attachment, beat the butter on high speed until creamy, about 1 minute. With the machine running, slowly dribble in the milk, occasionally stopping the machine and scraping down the sides of the bowl with a silicone spatula. The mixture should be fluffy, smooth, and shiny, like a buttercream frosting.

2 In a medium bowl, mix the flour, cracker crumbs, sugar, Parmesan, and pepper. With the mixer on low, add the flour mixture and mix just until the dough forms a mass on the paddle and the sides of the bowl are clean.

3 Gather up the dough and transfer to a lightly floured surface. Knead the dough a few times until it is smooth and supple. Divide it in half and shape into two 6-inch disks. Gently tap the sides of the disks on the work surface all around the circumference (this tamps the dough so the edges won't crack during rolling). Do not overhandle the dough.

4 Wrap the disks in plastic wrap and refrigerate until chilled, about 2 hours. The dough can also be chilled overnight, but it will be very hard and should stand at room temperature for about 30 minutes before rolling out. The wrapped dough can also be frozen in plastic freezer bags for up to 3 weeks. Defrost in the refrigerator overnight before rolling out.

Heirloom Tomato Crostata

Makes 6 to 8 servings

This free-form tart bakes a rainbow of juicy, ripe heirloom tomatoes into a basil-scented ricotta base for my take on a breakfast pizza. For the most flavorful crostata, look for just-picked ripe tomatoes at local farm stands. The toasted pine nuts add a crunchy counterpoint to the creamy, cheesy filling.

8 ounces (227 grams) heirloom tomatoes, preferably a mix of yellow, orange, and red, cut into ½-inch-thick slices

Kosher salt

1 cup (227 grams) fresh whole-milk ricotta cheese

1 large egg, beaten

1 teaspoon finely chopped fresh basil, plus thinly sliced leaves for garnish

Freshly ground black pepper

Unbleached all-purpose flour, for rolling the dough

1 disk (½ recipe) Classic Savory Dough (page 224)

3 ounces (85 grams) Monterey Jack cheese, coarsely grated (⅔ cup)

1 tablespoon finely grated Parmesan cheese

2 tablespoons pine nuts

Extra-virgin olive oil, for drizzling

Maldon sea salt, for sprinkling

1 Position a rack in the center of the oven and preheat to 375°F. Line a half-sheet pan with parchment paper.

2 Arrange the tomato slices in a single layer on a double thickness of paper towels. Sprinkle with kosher salt and let drain while you prepare the remaining ingredients, flipping the slices occasionally.

3 In a medium bowl, whisk the ricotta, egg, basil, and a pinch each of salt and pepper until well blended.

4 Lightly flour a work surface. Unwrap the dough and rap the entire circumference around its edge on the work surface. Dust the top of the dough with flour. Roll out into a 14-inch round. Transfer the dough to the prepared half-sheet pan. Pierce the dough in a uniform pattern with a fork.

5 Spread the ricotta mixture in the center of the dough, leaving a 2-inch border all around, and sprinkle the Monterey Jack on top of it. Pat the tomatoes dry and arrange in a single layer on top of the cheese. Sprinkle with the Parmesan, then the pine nuts. Pleat the 2-inch border of pastry over the filling.

6 Bake for 20 minutes. Reduce the oven temperature to 350°F and bake until the filling is set and the dough is cooked through, about 25 minutes longer. Let cool on a wire rack until warm or at room temperature.

7 To serve, drizzle oil on top of the crostata and sprinkle with the sliced basil, Maldon salt, and more pepper. Cut into wedges.

Provençal Quiche

Makes 6 to 8 servings

Like many cooks, I am helplessly in love with the flavors of Provence. Tomatoes, olives, basil, fennel, and goat cheese are some of my favorite cooking ingredients, and they seemed naturals for a quiche filling. This savory tart will put you in the mood for a glass of crisp rosé—if not a trip to the Riviera.

Unbleached all-purpose flour, for rolling the dough

1 disk (½ recipe) Black Pepper and Parmesan Savory Dough (page 225)

3 tablespoons freshly grated Parmesan cheese

1 tablespoon extra-virgin olive oil

1 cup (290 grams) very thinly sliced fennel

¼ cup (87 grams) thinly sliced shallots

1 small garlic clove, minced

1¼ cups (290 grams) heavy cream

1 tablespoon tomato paste

2 large eggs

¼ teaspoon fine sea salt

⅛ teaspoon freshly ground black pepper

1½ tablespoons unbleached all-purpose flour

3 ounces (85 grams) fresh goat cheese, such as Montrachet, crumbled

1 ripe plum tomato, seeded and cut into ½-inch dice

2 tablespoons pitted and coarsely chopped Kalamata olives

1 tablespoon chopped fresh basil

1 Position a rack in the lower third of the oven and preheat to 400°F.

2 On a lightly floured surface, roll out the dough into a ⅛-inch-thick circle. Following the instructions on page 223, line a 9-inch glass pie dish or a tart pan with a removable bottom with the dough. Prick the dough all over in a uniform pattern. Freeze for 15 minutes.

3 Line the dough with a 13-inch round of parchment paper and fill with pastry weights or dried beans. Place the dish on a half-sheet pan and bake for 10 minutes. Remove the paper and weights. Continue baking until the pastry is barely beginning to color, about 5 minutes longer. Remove from the oven and sprinkle the crust with 2 tablespoons Parmesan cheese. Let the crust cool completely in the pan on a wire rack. Reduce the oven temperature to 350°F.

4 Meanwhile, in a medium skillet, heat the oil over medium heat. Add the fennel and cook, stirring occasionally, until barely tender, about 4 minutes. Stir in the shallots and garlic and cook, breaking up the shallots into rings, until softened, about 2 minutes. Set aside.

5 In a 1-quart liquid measuring cup or a medium bowl, slowly whisk the cream into the tomato paste. Add the eggs, salt, and pepper. Sift in the flour and whisk until smooth.

6 Spread the fennel mixture in the crust. Sprinkle with the goat cheese, diced tomato, olives, and basil. Slowly pour in the cream mixture, distributing it evenly. Sprinkle with the remaining 1 tablespoon Parmesan cheese.

7 Return the pie dish, on the pan, to the oven and bake until the filling is puffed and golden brown, 30 to 35 minutes.

8 Cool the quiche for 10 minutes. Remove the sides of the pan if using a tart pan. Serve warm or at room temperature.

Arugula, Leek, and Shiitake Mushroom Quiche

Makes 6 to 8 servings

The sweetness of the leeks combines beautifully with peppery arugula and nutty Gruyère cheese in the filling for this quiche. Shiitakes are the surprise ingredient here. Their meaty, earthy flavor makes this an out-of-the-ordinary quiche that still tastes familiar and warming.

Unbleached all-purpose flour, for rolling the dough

1 disk (½ recipe) Classic Savory Dough (page 224)

4 tablespoons (114 grams) unsalted butter

6 ounces (170 grams) shiitake mushrooms, stems discarded, caps cut into ¼-inch-thick slices (2 cups)

1 small leek (4 ounces; 114 grams), white and pale green parts only, washed well and thinly sliced (¼ cup)

6 cups (174 grams) arugula, coarsely chopped

1¼ cups (290 grams) heavy cream

2 large egg yolks

¼ teaspoon fine sea salt

⅛ teaspoon freshly ground black pepper

Pinch of freshly grated nutmeg

1½ tablespoons unbleached all-purpose flour

4 ounces (114 grams) Gruyère cheese, coarsely grated (scant 1 cup)

2 tablespoons freshly grated Parmesan cheese

1 Position a rack in the lower third of the oven and preheat to 400°F.

2 On a lightly floured work surface, roll out the dough into a ⅛-inch-thick circle. Following the instructions on page 223, line a 9-inch glass pie dish or tart pan with a removable bottom with the dough. Using a fork, prick the dough all over in a uniform pattern. Freeze for 15 minutes.

3 Line the dough with a 13-inch round of parchment paper and fill with pastry weights or dried beans. Place the dish on a half-sheet pan and bake for 10 minutes. Remove the paper and weights. Continue baking until the pastry is barely beginning to color, about 5 minutes longer. Remove from the oven and let the crust cool completely in the dish on a wire rack. Reduce the oven temperature to 350°F.

4 Meanwhile, in a large skillet, heat 3 tablespoons butter over medium-high heat. Add the mushrooms and cook until wilted, about 4 minutes. Stir in the leek and cook until the mushrooms are tender, about 4 minutes longer. Transfer to a large bowl and set aside.

5 In the same skillet, heat the remaining 1 tablespoon butter over medium heat. Add the arugula and cook, stirring often, until completely wilted, about 2 minutes. Stir into the mushroom mixture.

6 In a 1-quart liquid measuring cup or a medium bowl, whisk the cream, egg yolks, salt, pepper, and nutmeg. Sift in the flour and whisk until smooth. Spread half of the Gruyère and half of the mushroom mixture in the crust. Sprinkle with the remaining Gruyère. Slowly pour in half of the cream mixture, distributing it evenly. Top with the remaining mushroom mixture, and then the remaining cream mixture. Sprinkle with the Parmesan cheese.

7 Return the pie dish, on the pan, to the oven. Bake until the top is puffed and golden brown and looks set when the sheet is shaken (only the very center of the filling will "jiggle"), about 30 minutes.

8 Cool the quiche for 10 minutes. Remove the sides of the pan if using a tart pan. Serve warm or at room temperature.

Spinach-Gruyère Quiche

Makes 6 to 8 servings

To highlight the flavors of the unique pepper-Parmesan crust, I keep this filling simple, with the classic combination of spinach and Gruyère. Simple certainly doesn't mean boring, though. You taste a range of cheesy flavors and textures in each bite. The melted Gruyère in the creamy custard filling gives way to a delightfully crunchy Parmesan crust.

Unbleached all-purpose flour, for rolling the dough

1 disk (½ recipe) Black Pepper and Parmesan Savory Dough (page 225)

1 tablespoon extra-virgin olive oil

1 medium garlic clove, minced

6 ounces (170 grams) spinach, tough stems removed, washed well

Fine sea salt and freshly ground black pepper

2 large eggs

1¼ cups (290 grams) heavy cream

⅛ teaspoon freshly grated nutmeg

1½ tablespoons unbleached all-purpose flour

4 ounces (114 grams) Gruyère cheese, coarsely grated (scant 1 cup)

3 tablespoons finely grated Parmesan cheese

1 Position a rack in the lower third of the oven and preheat to 375°F.

2 On a lightly floured surface, roll out the dough into a ⅛-inch-thick circle. Following the instructions on page 223, line a 9-inch glass pie dish or a tart pan with a removable bottom with the dough. Prick the dough all over with a fork in a uniform pattern. Freeze for 15 minutes.

3 Line the dough with a 13-inch round of parchment paper and fill with pastry weights or dried beans. Place the dish on a half-sheet pan and bake for 15 minutes. Remove the paper and weights. Continue baking until the pastry is barely beginning to color, about 5 minutes longer. Remove the dish and pan from the oven and let the crust cool completely in the dish on a wire rack. Reduce the oven temperature to 350°F.

4 Meanwhile, in a large skillet, heat the oil over medium heat. Add the garlic and cook, stirring, until golden, about 30 seconds. Stir in the spinach, season with salt and pepper, and cook, stirring, until wilted, about 2 minutes. Transfer to a cutting board and let cool slightly, then chop.

5 In a 1-quart liquid measuring cup or a medium bowl, whisk the eggs, cream, nutmeg, and a pinch each of salt and pepper. Sift in the flour and whisk until smooth.

6 Spread one-third of the Gruyère in the crust and top with half of the spinach mixture and 1 tablespoon Parmesan. Top with another third of the Gruyère, the remaining spinach, another tablespoon Parmesan, and

the remaining Gruyère. Slowly pour in the cream mixture, distributing it evenly. Sprinkle with the remaining 1 tablespoon Parmesan.

7 Return the pie dish, on the pan, to the oven. Bake until the filling is puffed and golden, 30 to 35 minutes.

8 Let the quiche cool for 10 minutes. Remove the sides of the pan if using a tart pan. Serve warm or at room temperature.

Feta Cheese and Spinach Hand Pies

Makes 8 individual pies

This version of spanakopita, Greek spinach pies, uses my tender yet sturdy savory crust instead of traditional flaky phyllo dough. This makes these little pies easy to pick up and eat out of hand at a casual get-together. Of course you can also serve these with knives and forks. The three-cheese filling, laced with fresh spinach, tastes delicious no matter how you dig in.

⅓ cup (87 grams) ricotta cheese

3 ounces (85 grams) feta cheese, coarsely crumbled (½ cup)

1 tablespoon finely grated Parmesan cheese

1 teaspoon minced fresh dill

⅛ teaspoon freshly grated nutmeg

2 large eggs

1 tablespoon extra-virgin olive oil

1 tablespoon minced onion

4 ounces (114 grams) baby spinach

Kosher salt and freshly ground black pepper

Unbleached all-purpose flour, for rolling out the dough

2 disks (1 recipe) Classic Savory Dough (page 224)

1 Position a rack in the lower third of the oven and preheat to 350°F. Line a half-sheet pan with parchment paper.

2 In a large bowl, stir the ricotta, feta, Parmesan, dill, nutmeg, and 1 egg until well combined. Set aside.

3 In a large skillet, heat the oil over medium-low heat until hot. Add the onion and cook, stirring often, until translucent, about 1 minute. Add the spinach, season with salt, and cook, stirring, until wilted, about 2 minutes. Transfer to a cutting board. Let cool slightly, then finely chop. Let cool completely. Fold the spinach into the cheese mixture and season to taste with pepper. Refrigerate until ready to use.

4 On a lightly floured surface, roll out the disks of dough, one at a time, to a ⅛-inch thickness. Using a 4¾-inch round cookie cutter, cut out 4 rounds from each portion of dough. (Or use a 4¾-inch plate as a guide to cut out the dough into rounds with a small sharp knife.) If you can't cut out 8 rounds from the dough, gather the scraps together, reroll, and cut out more rounds. Transfer the rounds to the prepared pan. Prick the dough all over with a fork in a uniform pattern. Refrigerate until firm, about 15 minutes.

5 In a small bowl, beat the remaining egg. Place 1 heaping tablespoon filling just off center on one dough round, leaving a ¾-inch border. Brush the border with the beaten egg, then fold the dough in half to enclose the filling and form a half-moon. Repeat with the remaining dough rounds and filling. Press the tines of a fork against the edges of each pie to seal. Brush the tops of the pies with the egg, then use the fork to prick the top of each pie 3 times.

6 Bake the pies until golden brown, about 25 minutes. Let cool slightly on the pan and serve warm.

Ham and Cheese Turnovers

Makes 8 turnovers

As much as I adore ham and cheese sandwiches, I don't think of them as brunch fare. Put the same filling in pastry, though, and I'll gladly enjoy one in the morning. The cheese in these turnovers melts into the buttery dough. To offset that richness, tangy pickles are enclosed in the ham and cheese.

Unbleached all-purpose flour, for rolling the dough

2 disks (1 recipe) Classic Savory Dough (page 224)

8 slices (4 ounces; 114 grams) aged sharp Cheddar cheese, cut into 4-inch squares

8 slices (6 ounces; 170 grams) best-quality ham

24 Bread-and-Butter Pickles (page 182), drained

1 large egg white, beaten

1 Position a rack in the lower third of the oven and preheat to 350°F. Line a half-sheet pan with parchment paper.

2 On a lightly floured surface, roll out one disk of dough into a 12-inch square. Use a sharp knife or pizza cutter to trim the edges to make a 10-inch square. Cut the square into four 5-inch squares. Prick the dough all over with a fork in a uniform pattern. Transfer to the prepared pan. Repeat with the remaining disk of dough, slightly overlapping the dough squares on the pan as needed. Refrigerate until firm, about 15 minutes.

3 Center 1 cheese slice on each dough square, leaving a ½-inch border on all sides. Top each with 1 ham slice, folded to match the size of the cheese, and 3 pickles, overlapping them slightly. Brush the borders with the egg white, then fold each dough square in half to enclose the filling and form a rectangle. Press the tines of a fork against the edges to seal. Brush the tops with the egg white, then use the fork to prick the top of each turnover 3 times.

4 Bake the turnovers until golden brown, about 25 minutes. Let cool slightly in the pan on a wire rack and serve hot, or serve warm.

Chapter Eleven

Potatoes, Meat, and Fish

SAVORY SIDE DISHES, FROM POTATOES TO MEATS AND FISH, SIGNAL A LEISURELY MORNING MEAL. THESE AREN'T THINGS YOU THROW TOGETHER for a fast weekday breakfast; they're recipes you take the time to make on weekends, when you're not rushing off somewhere. These tasty dishes elevate plates of eggs and baskets of breads and take them to the brunch time of day. (In fact, any of these recipes would also be welcome at lunch or dinner.) While some of them do take time to prepare, many of them can be made ahead of time. That makes entertaining early in the day easy.

KEY INGREDIENTS

Potatoes: Definitely go organic here, and be sure to buy the right variety. Boiling potatoes, such as red, fingerling, and Gold varieties, have a waxy flesh that stays firm after cooking. Baking potatoes, such as russet, Idaho, Long Island, and Burbank, have a high starch content that yields fluffy, relatively dry interiors when baked or fried. The starch also helps hold potato cakes together and keeps mashed potatoes fluffy.

Meats and Fish: Because these recipes don't require huge quantities of protein, you want to use the very best. Splurge on sustainably raised options if you can.

Three-Pepper Fingerling Potatoes

Makes 6 to 8 servings

These tasty potatoes with tricolor peppers have been a brunch mainstay ever since Sarabeth's opened. Everyone loves them. No matter how many servings we make, we are always hustling to make more toward the end of the shift. It is the simplicity of the dish that makes it such a favorite.

COOK'S NOTE: When prepping bell peppers, I always trim off the tops and bottoms, which are thicker and tougher than the rest of the pepper. I would rather have a little waste (or nibble the trimmings as a snack) than worry about some of the pepper strips taking longer to cook than others. After trimming the top and bottom, make a slit down one side of the pepper and unroll it into one long strip. Trim away the ribs and seeds. The pepper is now easy to cut into the desired shapes.

Kosher salt

3 pounds (1.4 kilograms) small fingerling potatoes, scrubbed and halved lengthwise

6 tablespoons (85 grams) Clarified Butter (page 54)

1 medium onion (5½ ounces; 156 grams), halved lengthwise and thinly sliced into half-moons

3 medium bell peppers (about 1 pound; 454 grams), 1 each red, orange, and yellow, cored, seeded, and cut into ¼-inch-wide strips (see Cook's Note)

Freshly ground black pepper

1 Bring a large pot of lightly salted water to a boil over high heat. Add the potatoes, return to a boil, and cook just until the potatoes are almost tender, about 10 minutes. Drain in a colander and rinse under cold water. Set aside. (The potatoes can be cooled, covered, and refrigerated for up to 1 day.)

2 In a large skillet, heat 3 tablespoons clarified butter over medium heat. Add the onion and bell peppers and cook, stirring occasionally, until the onion is golden, about 8 minutes. Transfer to a platter and set aside.

3 In the same skillet, heat the remaining 3 tablespoons clarified butter over medium heat. Add the potatoes and season with salt and black pepper. Cook, turning occasionally with a spatula, until the potatoes are lightly browned, about 8 minutes.

4 Gently stir the onion and pepper mixture into the potatoes and heat through. Serve hot.

Rakott Krumpli

Hungarian Potato and Egg Casserole

Makes 6 to 8 servings

This comforting casserole of potato and hard-boiled egg slices jumbled in a creamy sauce is one of the national dishes of Hungary. There it is usually eaten as a meatless main course, often for supper. It also makes a fine brunch or breakfast dish, accompanied by grilled sausages and a green salad.

COOK'S NOTE: Be sure to choose potatoes of similar size so they cook evenly.

4 large baking potatoes (3 pounds; 1.4 kilograms), such as russet, Idaho, or Burbank, scrubbed and halved crosswise

Kosher salt

1 tablespoon unsalted butter, at room temperature

12 large hard-boiled eggs (page 189), cut into ⅓-inch-thick slices

Freshly ground black pepper

3 cups (726 grams) sour cream

Sweet Hungarian paprika, for sprinkling

1 In a large pot, combine the potatoes with enough cold water to cover by 2 inches and bring to a boil over high heat. Lightly salt the water and cook until the potatoes are barely tender, about 35 minutes. Drain in a colander and rinse under cold running water until cool enough to handle. Peel the potatoes and cut into ½-inch-thick rounds.

2 Position a rack in the center of the oven and preheat to 350°F. Generously coat a 13 by 9 by 2-inch glass or ceramic baking dish with the butter.

3 Layer half of the potatoes evenly in the dish with no gaps, cutting the slices as needed to fit. Top with half of the eggs in an even layer. Generously season with salt and pepper. Dollop half of the sour cream on top, then spread it evenly with an offset spatula. Sprinkle with paprika. Repeat the layering with the remaining potatoes and eggs, more salt and pepper, and the remaining sour cream and paprika. Cover the dish with foil.

4 Bake until a knife inserted into the center of the casserole for 5 seconds comes out hot, about 45 minutes. Gently fold everything together to disperse the sauce evenly. Sprinkle with paprika and pepper and serve hot.

Potato Cake

Makes 4 to 6 servings

Golden brown and crispy, this potato cake hails from Switzerland, where it is called *rösti*. In America, you'd think of it as a giant hash brown. The entire surface and edges get nice and crisp, while the potato strands inside soften. The final sprinkling of salt brings another layer of tasty crunch. The potato cake needs to be turned halfway through cooking, which is easy to accomplish with a little confidence and a flat plate or lid. If the plate has a lip, the cake won't be as easy to flip.

COOK'S NOTE: Be sure to choose potatoes of similar size so they cook evenly. This recipe is best made with chilled potatoes, so boil them the night before serving and refrigerate them if you can.

3 medium baking potatoes (1 pound; 454 grams), such as russet, Idaho, or Burbank, scrubbed

Kosher salt and freshly ground black pepper

3 tablespoons Clarified Butter (page 54)

1 Prepare the potatoes at least 4 hours before serving: In a large pot, combine the potatoes with enough cold water to cover by 2 inches. Bring to a boil over high heat. Lightly salt the water and cook until the potatoes are barely tender, about 20 minutes. It's better to slightly undercook the potatoes at this point. Drain in a colander and rinse under cold running water until cool. Refrigerate until well chilled, at least 3½ hours, or, preferably, overnight.

2 Peel the potatoes. Grate them on the large holes of a box grater. Transfer to a large bowl and season with salt and pepper.

3 In a nonstick 8-inch skillet, heat 1½ tablespoons clarified butter over medium-high heat until very hot but not smoking. Add the potatoes. Using a spatula, spread the potatoes into an even layer and then press them into a compact cake. Reduce the heat to medium and cook until the potatoes look crispy around the edges, about 5 minutes.

4 Hold a flat plate or skillet lid tightly over the skillet and invert the plate and skillet together so the cake falls onto the plate. Heat the remaining 1½ tablespoons clarified butter in the skillet until very hot. Slide the potato cake back into the skillet and press firmly into a compact cake again, tucking in the edges to make a neat round. Cook until the underside is golden, about 5 minutes.

5 Slide the cake onto a serving plate and season with salt. Cut into wedges and serve hot.

Baked Bacon

Makes 4 to 6 servings

Almost everyone loves crisp bacon, but it can be a hassle, splattering up the stovetop no matter what you do. Baking is the sane way to cook bacon, especially for a crowd. If all of the bacon doesn't fit in a single layer on one half-sheet pan, use two pans on two oven racks and switch the position of the pans from top to bottom halfway through baking.

1 pound (454 grams) sliced bacon

1 Position a rack in the top third of the oven and preheat to 375°F. Line a half-sheet pan with parchment paper.

2 Arrange the bacon slices side by side on the prepared pan. Bake, without turning the slices, until cooked to the desired doneness, 15 to 20 minutes.

3 Transfer the bacon to paper towels to drain briefly, and serve hot.

Maple Bacon: Bake the bacon only until the fat is rendered, not until it's crisp, about 15 minutes. Very carefully drain all the fat from the pan, keeping the bacon in a single layer. Brush the bacon with ¼ cup (73 grams) pure maple syrup. Return to the oven and bake until the bacon is caramelized and crisp, 5 to 10 minutes longer. Drain on a wire rack or parchment paper and serve.

Bacon Twists: Thin-sliced bacon works best for these, as it tends to stick to itself. Wrap each bacon strip in a spiral around a long bamboo skewer. The bacon spirals should be about 6 inches long. Arrange the skewers on the prepared half-sheet pan. Cover with parchment paper and place a second half-sheet pan on top, bottom side down. Bake in a 325°F oven until crisp, about 20 minutes. Remove the top pan and paper, and carefully slide the bacon off the skewers onto paper towels. Drain briefly, and serve hot.

Herbed-Sausage Breakfast Sliders

Makes 8 sliders; 4 to 8 servings

These lightly herbed pork patties match my Water Mill Biscuits perfectly. Making your own sausage mix gives you control over the seasonings. Most supermarket ground pork is quite lean, so a dash of heavy cream helps keep the patties nice and moist.

SPECIAL EQUIPMENT: If you'd like to make these perfect rounds, for each patty, place 2¼ ounces (64 grams) meat mixture in a 2-inch-diameter ring mold and poke down with your fingers, to avoid compacting the meat too tightly, then lift off the ring mold.

1 pound (454 grams) ground pork
2 tablespoons finely chopped shallots
2 tablespoons heavy cream
2 teaspoons finely chopped fresh flat-leaf parsley
1 teaspoon finely chopped fresh thyme
½ teaspoon finely chopped fresh rosemary
½ teaspoon finely chopped fresh sage
½ teaspoon kosher salt
⅛ teaspoon freshly ground black pepper
1 tablespoon extra-virgin olive oil
½ cup (133 grams) Plum Ketchup (page 174)
8 Water Mill Biscuits (page 118), split
½ cup (10 grams) baby greens
24 Bread-and-Butter Pickles (page 182)

1 In a medium bowl, combine the pork, shallots, cream, parsley, thyme, rosemary, sage, salt, and pepper. Mix with your hands until well combined. Shape the mixture into eight 2-inch patties.

2 In a large skillet, heat the oil over medium heat. Add the patties and cook, turning once, until browned and cooked through, about 12 minutes.

3 Spread the ketchup on the biscuit bottoms, then top with the greens, sausage patties, and pickles. Sandwich with the biscuit tops and serve hot.

Apple-Sausage Crumble

Makes 6 to 8 servings

Let me be honest: This is not the most attractive dish. It all ends up brown and a bit lumpy—but it tastes great. And that's what really matters. Italian sausages are browned to a crisp, then stirred into buttery spiced sweet-tart apples to coat them with their juices. The crumble is delicious on its own, but it's even more satisfying with eggs. You could stuff it into an omelet, mix it into a frittata, or fold it into scrambled eggs.

1 tablespoon Clarified Butter (page 54)

1 pound (454 grams) sweet Italian sausages, cut into ½-inch-thick slices

2 tablespoons unsalted butter

2 Granny Smith apples (12 ounces; 340 grams), peeled, cored, and cut into ½-inch pieces (3 cups)

Pinch of ground cinnamon

Pinch of freshly grated nutmeg

Kosher salt and freshly ground black pepper, if needed

1 In a large skillet, heat the clarified butter over medium-high heat until hot. Add the sausage and cook, turning occasionally, until cooked through and lightly browned, about 5 minutes. Transfer to a plate and set aside. Drain and discard the fat from the pan.

2 Add the unsalted butter to the skillet and melt over medium heat. Add the apples and cook, stirring occasionally, until barely tender, about 5 minutes.

3 Stir in the reserved sausage and season with the cinnamon and nutmeg. Season with salt and pepper if needed. Serve hot.

Grilled Ham
with Orange-Maple Glaze

Makes 4 to 6 servings

If you're the kind of person who can't imagine eggs without a side of ham, this easy recipe will be a revelation. It uses a thick ham slice, which can be found prepackaged in the supermarket meat case. A simple marinade of fresh orange juice and maple syrup helps draw out excess salt from the ham and then cooks into a tasty glaze.

One 1-pound (454-gram) cooked ham slice, preferably bone-in

⅔ cup (149 grams) fresh orange juice

2 tablespoons pure maple syrup

Freshly ground black pepper

Vegetable oil, for the pan

1 Rinse the ham under cold running water and pat dry with paper towels. In a shallow glass or ceramic dish, whisk the orange juice and syrup and season with pepper. Add the ham slice and turn to coat. Cover with plastic wrap and refrigerate, turning the ham occasionally, for at least 1 hour, or up to overnight.

2 Position the broiler rack 6 inches from the heat source and preheat the broiler. Line the broiler pan with foil. Lightly oil the broiler pan rack.

3 Remove the ham from the marinade and place on the rack. Broil, turning once, until glazed on both sides, 6 to 8 minutes. Slice the ham and serve hot.

Roasted Chicken and Fennel Patties

Makes 16 patties; 8 to 10 servings

Here I combined the concept of corned beef hash with sausage patties, then lightened up both without sacrificing flavor. Roasted chicken can hold its own in savory depth against cured meats, but it tastes fresher. It's the ideal match for a blend of green vegetables and herbs. The hash mixture takes an elegant turn when formed into compact patties. They're moist and flavorful and especially good with poached or scrambled eggs (page 192 or 195). Serve them with freshly baked Water Mill Biscuits (page 118) and salad for a classy brunch.

COOK'S NOTES: If you don't have leftover roasted chicken on hand, you can use a rotisserie chicken. Just be sure to buy a high-quality, minimally seasoned bird. The chicken and potatoes should be chopped into very small pieces or the hash won't hold together. Though you may be tempted to use a food processor, the texture will suffer: Use a sharp heavy chef's knife. Chilled potatoes make the best cubes, so try to cook the potatoes the night before and refrigerate them overnight.

4 fingerling potatoes (10½ ounces; 298 grams), scrubbed

Kosher salt

8 tablespoons (110 grams) extra-virgin olive oil

½ cup (87 grams) very finely chopped fennel

¼ cup (33 grams) finely chopped celery heart (strings removed with a vegetable peeler before chopping)

2 tablespoons finely chopped scallions

8 ounces (227 grams) roasted chicken meat, cut into ¼-inch pieces (1½ cups)

2 tablespoons finely chopped fresh flat-leaf parsley

⅓ cup (77 grams) mayonnaise

¼ cup (58 grams) heavy cream

1 large egg, beaten

1¼ cups (113 grams) dry bread crumbs

Freshly ground black pepper

1 In a medium pot, combine the potatoes with enough cold water to cover by 2 inches and bring to a boil over high heat. Lightly salt the water and cook until the potatoes are tender when pierced with a knife, about 20 minutes. Drain in a colander and rinse under cold running water until cool enough to handle. If you have time, refrigerate until chilled, or up to overnight, in an airtight container.

2 Peel the potatoes and cut into ¼-inch cubes.

3 In a large skillet, heat 2 tablespoons oil over medium heat. Add the fennel, celery, and scallions. Season with salt and cook, stirring occasionally, until tender, about 5 minutes. Transfer to a large bowl and let cool slightly, then add the potatoes, chicken, parsley, mayonnaise, cream, egg, ¼ cup bread crumbs, ¼ teaspoon salt, and ⅛ teaspoon pepper. Gently fold until well mixed.

4 Shape the mixture into sixteen 2-inch patties. Spread the remaining 1 cup bread crumbs in a shallow dish. Gently press both sides of each patty in the crumbs to coat.

5 In a large skillet, heat 3 tablespoons oil over medium heat. Add half of the patties and cook, turning once, until browned on both sides, 8 to 10 minutes. Adjust the heat as needed so the crumbs don't burn. Serve immediately, or keep warm on a parchment paper–lined half-sheet pan in a 200°F oven while you cook the second batch. Repeat with the remaining 3 tablespoons oil and patties. Serve hot.

Double Salmon Rillettes

Makes 8 servings

When I made this dish for the first time again after many years, all I could say was, "Wow." I had forgotten how delicious and luscious the spread is. Wine-poached fresh salmon and smoked salmon are blended into butter brightened with a squeeze of lime juice. I like to serve this elegant dish with toast points or Knekkebrød (page 45).

2 tablespoons Clarified Butter (page 54)
¼ cup (35 grams) finely chopped shallots
Two 5-ounce (142-gram) boneless, skinless salmon fillets
¼ cup (56 grams) dry white wine
4 ounces (114 grams) smoked salmon, finely diced
8 tablespoons (114 grams) unsalted butter, cut into 8 pieces, at room temperature
2 tablespoons extra-virgin olive oil
2 tablespoons fresh lime juice
Kosher salt and freshly ground black pepper

1 In a medium skillet, heat the clarified butter over medium-low heat. Add the shallots and cook, stirring often, just until softened, about 2 minutes. Add the salmon fillets and wine. Cover and cook until the salmon is opaque throughout, about 10 minutes.

2 Using a slotted spatula, transfer the salmon to a large bowl. Bring the pan juices to a boil over high heat and boil until reduced to 3 tablespoons, about 1 minute. Pour over the salmon. Let cool completely.

3 With a fork, flake the cooked salmon into ¾-inch pieces. Fold in the smoked salmon. Transfer two-thirds of the salmon mixture to a food processor, along with the butter. Pulse until the butter is incorporated. Add the oil and lime juice and pulse until combined. The mixture should still be slightly chunky. Return the mixture to the bowl with the remaining salmon and gently fold together. Season with salt and pepper.

4 Transfer the rillettes to a serving bowl, cover tightly with plastic wrap, and refrigerate until well chilled, at least 2 hours, or up to overnight. Serve cold.

Three-Herb Gravlax

Makes 12 to 16 servings

Gravlax is the magical transformation of raw salmon into gossamer cured ribbons. The preparation is simple. The essentials are time (largely unattended), a beautiful piece of salmon, coarse salt, sugar, and lots of fresh herbs. I puree enough mint, basil, and dill to turn the cure a bright emerald green. The classic way to serve gravlax is with thinly sliced black bread and a sweet mustard sauce, as here, but try it with bagels and cream cheese or scrambled eggs (page 195).

COOK'S NOTE: Salmon fillets usually have tiny pin bones that must be removed before cooking. Professional cooks always have a pair of tweezers reserved for this job. If you don't have a spare pair of tweezers for the task, use a small sharp knife to help you locate the bones and then press the bone between the side (not the edge) of the blade and your thumb, to act as makeshift pliers.

1 cup (44 grams) coarsely chopped fresh mint, plus a few sprigs for garnish

1 cup (45 grams) coarsely chopped fresh basil, plus a few sprigs for garnish

1 cup (50 grams) coarsely chopped fresh dill, plus a few sprigs for garnish

2 cups (283 grams) kosher salt

2 cups (400 grams) granulated sugar

One 3-pound (1.4-kilogram) skin-on salmon fillet, deboned, rinsed, and patted dry

2 tablespoons whole black peppercorns

2 tablespoons fennel seeds

Mustard Sauce

1 cup (240 grams) Dijon mustard • ¼ cup (73 grams) pure maple syrup

Thinly sliced black bread, for serving

Capers, drained and rinsed, for serving

Edible flowers, for garnish

1 In a food processor, process the mint, basil, and dill with 1 cup salt and 1 cup sugar until the herbs are completely pureed. The mixture will have a beautiful green color and the texture of finely crushed ice. Transfer to a large bowl and stir in the remaining 1 cup salt and 1 cup sugar. Mix well.

2 You will need two half-sheet pans, one to rest the fish on and one to cover the fish. Line one pan with parchment paper and spread half of the salt mixture on it in a thick layer slightly larger than the fillet. Place the fillet

on top, skin side down, and sprinkle with the peppercorns and fennel seeds. Cover completely with the remaining salt mixture, packing it tightly onto the fillet. Cover the fillet completely with plastic wrap.

3 Place the other half-sheet pan, bottom side down, on top of the fillet. Weigh the top sheet pan with a few heavy cans and refrigerate for 24 to 36 hours. The length of the cure will give different results: A short cure will yield gravlax that has a light herbal flavor and a texture close to that of sushi. A longer cure will give a deeper herb flavor and a drier result, similar to smoked salmon.

4 On the day of serving, make the mustard sauce: In a small bowl, stir the mustard and maple syrup. Cover and refrigerate for at least 1 hour before serving.

5 Unwrap the gravlax and remove from the salt mixture. Lightly rinse under cold running water to remove the spices and cure, drain well, and pat dry with paper towels. The gravlax can be tightly wrapped in plastic wrap and refrigerated for up to 2 days.

6 To serve, hold a long, thin sharp knife at a sharp diagonal and thinly slice the salmon flesh off the skin. Arrange the slices attractively on a platter. Garnish with the fresh herb sprigs. Serve cold, with the mustard sauce, bread, onions, and capers.

Crunchy Crab Cakes
with Tartar Sauce

Makes 6 crab cakes

Crab cakes should taste like crab, not filler. To that end, these plump cakes use just a bit of bread crumbs as a binder, along with some well-chosen vegetables and seasonings. There are so many ways to serve these crab cakes, it's hard to pick a favorite. They're wonderful by themselves with tartar sauce and a lemon wedge, on a green salad with lemony vinaigrette, alongside an omelet, or tucked into a soft brioche roll, slathered with that tartar sauce. I especially like them with my Zesty Vegetable Slaw with Buttermilk Dressing (page 274). Have fun finding out which way you prefer.

COOK'S NOTE: Old Bay seasoning, a commercial blend of different herbs and spices well suited to crab, is available at most supermarkets and at specialty food stores.

SPECIAL EQUIPMENT: If you'd like to make these perfect rounds, use a 2½-inch-diameter ice-cream scoop to place each portion of crab mixture into a 3-inch ring mold and press down firmly, then lift off the ring mold.

Tartar Sauce

1 cup (231 grams) mayonnaise
2 tablespoons finely chopped cornichons
2 teaspoons capers, drained and rinsed
2 teaspoons finely chopped fresh flat-leaf parsley

2½ tablespoons mayonnaise
1 tablespoon heavy cream
2 teaspoons whole-grain Dijon mustard
¼ teaspoon Old Bay seasoning (see Cook's Note)
8 ounces (227 grams) lump crabmeat, picked over for shells and cartilage
1½ tablespoons finely diced celery heart (strings removed with a vegetable peeler before chopping)
2 teaspoons finely chopped scallion
1 teaspoon very finely chopped fresh mint
1 teaspoon very finely chopped fresh flat-leaf parsley
1 cup plus 1 tablespoon (57 grams) panko bread crumbs
Kosher salt and freshly ground black pepper
¼ cup (39 grams) fine semolina flour
2 tablespoons Clarified Butter (page 54)

Garnishes

Finely chopped cornichons

Capers, drained and rinsed

Microgreens

1 To make the tartar sauce: In a medium bowl, mix the mayonnaise, cornichons, capers, and parsley. Cover and refrigerate for at least 1 hour, or up to 2 days, to blend the flavors.

2 Meanwhile, make the crab cakes: In a large bowl, stir the mayonnaise, cream, mustard, and Old Bay seasoning together. Add the crabmeat, celery, scallion, mint, and parsley. Sprinkle with 1 tablespoon panko and toss lightly until well mixed. Season to taste with salt and pepper.

3 Gently form the crab mixture into 6 patties, each about 3 inches in diameter and 1 inch thick. In a shallow dish, combine the semolina and the remaining 1 cup panko. Dredge each crab cake in the crumbs to coat, shaking off excess, and transfer to a plate. Cover and refrigerate until firm, about 1 hour.

4 To cook the crab cakes: In a nonstick large skillet, heat 1 tablespoon clarified butter over medium heat. Add 3 crab cakes and cook, turning once, until golden brown on both sides, 6 to 8 minutes. Drain on paper towels. Repeat with the remaining 1 tablespoon clarified butter and 3 crab cakes.

5 Serve hot, garnished with cornichons, capers, and microgreens. Pass the tartar sauce on the side.

Chapter Twelve

Soups and Salads

FROM THE INCEPTION OF THIS BOOK, I DEBATED ABOUT WHETHER OR NOT TO INCLUDE SOUP AND SALAD RECIPES. THEY DON'T SOUND LIKE STANDARD breakfast foods, but they are welcome at brunch. Soup rounds out a meal of lighter fare, while salad balances the richness of heartier dishes.

I've never even met the people who finally convinced me to include this chapter. They're the loyal customers who wrote to me, asking why I hadn't published my tomato soup recipe in my last cookbook. I couldn't let them down. And I have to agree with them: Our signature Velvety Cream of Tomato Soup is a must-have recipe. So too are the other soups here. All can be served in large portions as main dishes, but I like to offer small shots of them in the morning.

The salads are much the same. A small serving on the side is just enough as part of a large menu, while a generous plate can be the centerpiece of a light brunch. Both the soups and salads rely on fresh produce. Use only the best seasonal vegetables, preferably organic and from local farms. Needless to say, all of these dishes would be welcome at any time of day.

Good Morning Gazpacho

Makes about 10 cups

Spain's national soup may just be the ultimate summer refresher. To customize the classic for brunch, I add Bloody Mary seasonings. The bite of horseradish and the complex saltiness of Worcestershire accentuate the savory crunch of the summer vegetables. I like my gazpacho very, very chunky. If you prefer a soupier mixture, simply add more tomato juice.

4 ripe beefsteak tomatoes (11¾ ounces; 333 grams), cored, halved, seeded, and cut into ¼-inch dice (2 cups)

1 large cucumber (6¾ ounces; 191 grams), peeled, halved lengthwise, seeded, and cut into ¼-inch dice (1 cup)

1 medium green bell pepper (5 ounces; 142 grams), cored, seeds and ribs removed, and cut into ¼-inch dice (⅔ cup)

1 medium red bell pepper (5 ounces; 142 grams), cored, seeds and ribs removed, and cut into ¼-inch dice (⅔ cup)

1 medium celery heart rib (2½ ounces; 71 grams), strings removed with a vegetable peeler and rib cut into ¼-inch dice (½ cup)

½ medium Vidalia onion (2¾ ounces; 78 grams), finely chopped (½ cup)

6 cups (1.4 kilograms) bottled tomato juice

2 tablespoons fresh lemon juice

1 tablespoon Worcestershire sauce

2 tablespoons cherry or regular balsamic vinegar

2 tablespoons freshly grated horseradish or drained prepared horseradish

2 teaspoons kosher salt, or to taste

¼ teaspoon freshly ground black pepper, or to taste

10 dashes Tabasco sauce, or to taste

Lemon slices, for garnish

3 tablespoons coarsely chopped fresh cilantro

1 In a large bowl, mix the tomatoes, cucumber, green and red bell peppers, celery, onion, tomato juice, lemon juice, Worcestershire sauce, vinegar, horseradish, salt, black pepper, and Tabasco sauce. Taste and adjust the seasonings if necessary. Transfer the gazpacho to a storage container, cover tightly with plastic wrap, and refrigerate until well chilled, at least 2 hours, or up to 8 hours.

2 To serve, ladle the gazpacho into serving glasses—which can range from shot glasses to tall tumblers (photo page 265, middle). Cut a slit in one side of each lemon slice, dip the slice into the chopped cilantro, and hook the slice over the lip of the glass as a garnish. Serve immediately, with long spoons if needed.

Chilled Borscht

Makes about 10 cups

Borscht is a traditional Russian beet soup, usually prepared with beef and served steaming hot. In America, it's become synonymous with jarred borscht, which contains little more than bland beets. I prefer mine cold and made with so many beets that you almost need a fork to eat it. To accentuate the natural sweetness of the beets and achieve a yin-yang sweet-tart balance, I simmer them with both apple and pomegranate juices. I skip the beef, but I use chicken stock to add body and sour cream for richness. The resulting soup is simultaneously refreshing and satisfying, and it's delicious any time of year.

1½ tablespoons extra-virgin olive oil

1 medium Vidalia onion (5½ ounces; 156 grams), halved lengthwise and thinly sliced into half-moons (1 cup)

2 medium celery heart ribs (5 ounces; 142 grams), strings removed with a vegetable peeler and thinly sliced (1 cup)

1½ pounds (680 grams) red beets

4 cups (896 grams) homemade chicken stock or store-bought low-sodium chicken broth

2 cups (448 grams) water

1 cup (224 grams) unsweetened apple juice

1 cup (224 grams) lightly sweetened pomegranate juice

2 tablespoons apple cider vinegar

1½ tablespoons packed light brown sugar

1 teaspoon kosher salt

⅛ teaspoon freshly ground black pepper

1 tablespoon cherry or regular balsamic vinegar

1 tablespoon fresh lemon juice

1 cup (242 grams) sour cream, plus more for serving

Small fresh dill sprigs, for garnish

1 In a large pot, heat the oil over medium-low heat. Add the onion and celery and cook, stirring occasionally, until very tender, about 10 minutes.

2 Meanwhile, peel the beets and cut into large chunks. Using a food processor fitted with the coarse grating blade or a box grater, coarsely grate the beets.

3 Add the beets to the pot, along with the stock, water, apple juice, pomegranate juice, cider vinegar, brown sugar, salt, and pepper. Bring to a boil over high heat, then reduce the heat to medium-low and simmer until the beets are just tender, about 30 minutes.

4 Remove the borscht from the heat and stir in the balsamic vinegar and lemon juice. Let cool completely, then cover and refrigerate until well chilled, at least 4 hours, or up to overnight.

5 Transfer 2 cups of the liquid from the soup (without beets) to a liquid measuring cup. Place the sour cream in a medium bowl and gradually whisk in the 2 cups soup until very smooth; if there are any lumps in the sour cream mixture, strain through a fine-mesh sieve. Stir the sour cream mixture into the soup.

6 Divide the soup among chilled shot glasses or other glasses or bowls (photo below, left). Top each serving with a dollop of the sour cream and garnish with dill.

Velvety Cream of Tomato Soup

Makes about 15 cups

This soup is so good that customers come to our restaurants just to have a bowl. It is my favorite savory soup, and it's been a draw since I first served it decades ago at my restaurant. As is true of many great inventions, its current incarnation was the result of a few happy accidents. When I created the recipe, I sent a young cook out to buy onions for me. He came back with shallots, not knowing the difference. I found that the addition made the result even more delicious. A few years later, a collision in the kitchen caused the cheese for an omelet filling to drop into a bowl of soup. When a server took a spoonful, he said, "Sara, you have to taste this." I took one slurp and went crazy for it.

COOK'S NOTE: Be sure to buy canned tomatoes packed in puree, *not juice*. I prefer to tear, not chop, the dill. *Do not add salt while the soup is cooking, as it will cause the soup to curdle.* If that should happen, combine ½ cup whole milk and ½ cup heavy cream and add to the soup while whisking vigorously.

6 tablespoons (85 grams) unsalted butter

½ medium Vidalia onion (2¾ ounces; 78 grams) chopped (½ cup)

2 medium shallots (4 ounces; 114 grams), chopped (½ cup)

Greens from 4 scallions, thinly sliced (½ cup)

3 medium garlic cloves, minced

Two 28-ounce (793-gram) cans diced tomatoes in puree

4 cups (896 grams) whole milk, or as needed

4 cups (928 grams) heavy cream

⅓ cup (47 grams) unbleached all-purpose flour

Fine sea salt and freshly ground black pepper

About ⅓ cup (17 grams) fresh dill fronds, torn into tiny sprigs (see Cook's Note)

4 ounces (114 grams) white Cheddar cheese, shredded (1 cup)

1 In a large skillet, melt 2 tablespoons butter over medium-low heat. Add the onion, shallots, scallion greens, and garlic. Cook, stirring occasionally, until the vegetables have softened and are translucent, about 4 minutes.

2 Transfer the mixture to the top of a large double boiler and place over the bottom pan of boiling water. (You can also use a Dutch oven, but you will need to stir frequently and cook at a lower temperature to prevent scorching and curdling.) Add the tomatoes with their puree, the milk, and cream and bring to a simmer, stirring often.

3 Meanwhile, in a small saucepan, melt the remaining 4 tablespoons butter over low heat. Gradually whisk in the flour to make a roux and cook, whisking constantly, for 3 minutes, being sure the roux doesn't brown. Whisk about 1½ cups of the hot tomato mixture into the roux, then pour the mixture into the soup and stir until blended. Reduce the heat to low and simmer the soup, stirring occasionally, for about 35 minutes to blend the flavors and thicken the soup.

4 Remove the top of the double boiler (or the Dutch oven) from the heat and add the dill. Season to taste with salt and pepper. (The soup can be prepared up to 2 days ahead, cooled completely, covered, and refrigerated. It will thicken when chilled. If you'd like a thinner soup, stir in a touch of milk after the soup is completely heated through. Do not freeze the soup.)

5 Serve hot, in a bowl or cup (photo page 265, right), topping each serving with shredded cheese.

Sarabeth's Salad Primer

A SALAD ISN'T ABOUT A RECIPE FOR THE VEGETABLES AND ADD-INS—IT'S ABOUT THE DRESSING. YOU REALLY NEED ONLY TWO GREAT, VERSATILE dressings: a classic vinaigrette and a delicious creamy dressing. I've provided those on pages 270 and 271. As for the salad itself, it can be a simple mound of greens to serve with your eggs or it can grow into anything and become a complete meal. There are only a few things to keep in mind when composing a salad.

First, think about the people you're serving. Some people are very into the greenery, others need nuts, and others crave fruit. My kids have got to have cucumbers and red, orange, and yellow peppers. You may love olives in your salad and wonder, "Who doesn't love olives?" I'll tell you who: some of my grandchildren. So I always keep the olives on the side when they're around.

The next thing to consider is the greens. Not all salads have to have greens, but those that do should have really good ones. If you're like me, you like a lot of mixed greens. If you're going to have a one-green salad—whether it's kale, spinach, or arugula—go straight to the farm for the most flavorful greens. Otherwise, you'll just be eating a pile of bland leaves. Then there are salads where you want a little chiffonade of mint or basil to provide accents of fresh herbs. You can even go ahead and mix every lettuce under the sun, from radicchio to endive. You can do your thing with greens.

Vegetable choices should start with the season. Get whatever's best and fresh at the farmers' market. Look for a variety of colors, textures, shapes, and, of course, flavors. But even a mix of tomatoes can have a huge range of tastes. Be sure to prep the vegetables properly. For example, radishes are great, but there's nothing worse than biting into a big chunk of one in a salad. Get out the mandoline and do super-thin slices. (That goes for fennel too.)

If you're a salad person like me, you should also stock your pantry and refrigerator with additions that keep. I always have raisins, dried cranberries, candied lemon peel, apples, toasted nuts, and candied nuts on hand. If I've made a batch of grains like wheat berries (page 32), bulgur, or couscous, I'll save the leftovers for salad.

Whatever else you toss in, a little piece of cheese takes a salad to the next level. My favorites include crumbled French sheep's-milk feta, shaved Gruyère, and good, hard Parmesan grated to a dust or peeled into shavings.

It's essential to dress a salad at the last minute. My mom used to pour the dressing into the bottom of the salad bowl and then build and toss the salad right before we dug in. You can, of course, always drizzle the dressing on top too—just not a second too soon. As soon as your salad is dressed, eat and enjoy.

Citrus Vinaigrette

Makes about 1½ cups

Adding orange juice to a classic lemon vinaigrette brings a welcome, subtle sweetness. Balsamic vinegar echoes the natural sugary notes. I use white balsamic to avoid discoloring the dressing, and sometimes I choose unseasoned rice vinegar.

¼ cup (56 grams) fresh orange juice
3 tablespoons fresh lemon juice
1 tablespoon white balsamic vinegar
1 teaspoon Dijon mustard
1 teaspoon superfine sugar
Kosher salt and freshly ground black pepper
¾ cup (165 grams) canola oil
¼ cup (55 grams) extra-virgin olive oil

In a blender, combine the orange juice, lemon juice, vinegar, mustard, sugar, and a pinch each of salt and pepper and puree until smooth. In a liquid measuring cup, combine the canola and olive oils. With the blender running, add the oil mixture in a slow, steady stream through the feed tube and continue blending until emulsified. Season to taste with salt and pepper. The vinaigrette can be refrigerated in an airtight container for up to 3 days.

Buttermilk Dressing

Makes about 1½ cups

Tangy buttermilk keeps my go-to creamy dressing light. Cider vinegar thins the mixture, while celery seeds and fresh dill punch up the seasonings. Celery seeds take time to soften and impart their flavor, so the dressing needs to sit for a while before being used. This dressing stands up to bold greens and will become a favorite. I've been known to bring a bottle of it to friends as a gift.

- *½ cup (121 grams) sour cream*
- *½ cup (116 grams) mayonnaise*
- *½ cup (112 grams) low-fat buttermilk*
- *4 teaspoons apple cider vinegar*
- *2 teaspoons pure maple syrup*
- *¾ teaspoon celery seeds*
- *1 teaspoon chopped fresh dill*
- *½ teaspoon Worcestershire sauce*
- *¾ teaspoon kosher salt*
- *⅛ teaspoon freshly ground black pepper*

In a medium bowl, combine all of the ingredients and whisk until well blended. Cover and refrigerate for at least 2 hours before serving. The dressing can be refrigerated in an airtight container for up to 3 days.

Cucumber and Tomato Salad
with Honey-Grapefruit Vinaigrette

Makes 6 servings

Crunchy and fresh, this summer salad works especially well with savory egg dishes. Cherry tomatoes are just juicy enough and parsley delivers a fresh finish. The soy sauce and sesame oil in the subtly sweet grapefruit dressing bring a surprising pop of Asian flavors.

8 Persian or other mini cucumbers (1⅓ pounds; 605 grams), halved lengthwise, seeded, and cut into ½-inch-thick half-moons

1½ teaspoons kosher salt

1 pint (1 pound; 454 grams) cherry tomatoes, halved lengthwise

1 small red onion (2¾ ounces; 78 grams), thinly sliced

2 tablespoons chopped fresh flat-leaf parsley

Vinaigrette

½ cup (112 grams) fresh grapefruit juice

2 tablespoons ketchup

2 tablespoons honey

1 tablespoon reduced-sodium soy sauce

1 tablespoon red wine vinegar

1 teaspoon finely chopped peeled fresh ginger

1 small garlic clove, finely chopped

⅓ cup (73 grams) peanut oil

⅓ cup (73 grams) canola oil

1 tablespoon sesame oil

Kosher salt and freshly ground black pepper

1 In a colander set over a bowl, toss the cucumbers with the salt. Let stand for 30 minutes. Rinse the cucumbers well under cold water and drain. Transfer to paper towels to drain, spread them out in a single layer, and cover with more paper towels. Lightly press on the cucumbers to remove excess moisture.

2 To make the vinaigrette: In a blender, combine the grapefruit juice, ketchup, honey, soy sauce, vinegar, ginger, and garlic and puree until well blended. In a liquid measuring cup, combine the peanut, canola, and sesame oils. With the blender running, add the oil mixture in a slow, steady stream through the feed tube and continue blending until emulsified. Season to taste with salt and pepper.

3 In a large bowl, gently toss the cucumbers with the tomatoes, onion, and parsley. Drizzle enough vinaigrette to lightly coat and toss again. Cover the salad and refrigerate for at least 30 minutes, or up to 1½ hours. Toss again just before serving. Any extra vinaigrette can be refrigerated in an airtight container for up to 3 days.

Zesty Vegetable Slaw
with Buttermilk Dressing

Makes 8 servings

In lieu of the classic green cabbage, I make my slaw with softer, tastier Savoy leaves. Thin matchsticks of celery root, fennel, and carrot deliver flavor-filled crunch. The slaw tastes best after marinating for at least 2 hours, making it an ideal dish for entertaining. I especially enjoy this slaw with Crunchy Crab Cakes with Tartar Sauce (page 257).

SPECIAL EQUIPMENT: A mandoline, whether French or Japanese, is the best tool for quickly slicing hard vegetables into perfect matchsticks. You can also julienne the vegetables by hand with a very sharp chef's knife.

1 large celery root (1 pound; 454 grams), trimmed and well peeled

1 small fennel bulb (12 ounces; 340 grams), trimmed and cored

2 large carrots (12 ounces; 340 grams), trimmed and peeled

½ small head Savoy cabbage (8 ounces; 227 grams), cored and shredded

1 tablespoon poppy seeds

Buttermilk Dressing (page 271)

Kosher salt and freshly ground black pepper

1 Using the julienne blade of a mandoline or a very sharp knife, cut the celery root, fennel, and carrots into thin matchsticks. Transfer to a large bowl, add the cabbage and poppy seeds, and toss well to mix. Add the dressing and toss until evenly coated. Season to taste with salt and pepper. Cover the slaw and refrigerate for at least 2 hours, or up to 1 day.

2 To serve, toss the slaw and season to taste again. Serve cold.

Morning Crudités
with Green Goddess Dipping Sauce

Makes 8 to 12 servings (makes about 1½ cups sauce)

At the height of summer, I love blending fragrant basil leaves into this creamy sauce. Anchovies are a signature ingredient in green goddess sauce and should not be omitted. If you think you don't like them, try them again—they're wonderful here. Any vegetables that taste good raw can be used for crudités. Choose whatever seasonal items look best at the market. You can also use this dipping sauce as a salad dressing for leafy greens.

Dipping Sauce

¾ cup (174 grams) mayonnaise

⅔ cup (20 grams) lightly packed coarsely chopped fresh basil

Greens from 3 scallions, thinly sliced (⅓ cup)

3 tablespoons fresh lemon juice

1 small garlic clove, chopped

2 jarred anchovy fillets, rinsed and patted dry

1 teaspoon kosher salt

⅛ teaspoon freshly ground black pepper

¾ cup (182 grams) sour cream

Crudités, such as radishes, sugar snap peas, rainbow carrots, and cucumbers, for serving

1 To make the dipping sauce: In a food processor, combine the mayonnaise, basil, scallion greens, lemon juice, garlic, anchovies, salt, and pepper and process until smooth, scraping down the sides of the bowl as necessary. Transfer to a medium bowl. Use a large whisk to fold the sour cream into the mixture. The dipping sauce can be refrigerated in an airtight container for up to 3 days.

2 Serve the crudités with the chilled sauce.

Index

Pages numbers in *italics* indicate illustrations.

D

E

F

G

H

Acknowledgments

It seems like yesterday that I opened the first Sarabeth's and started flipping pancakes, shaping fluffy omelets, filling our cases with freshly baked pastries, and stirring bubbling pots of my legendary fruit spreads. I am so grateful to our customers who have made it possible for me to continue doing what I love. Your praises and loyalty will always be the defining ingredient of our success.

I am the luckiest person on the planet to have the greatest husband and business partner one could ever wish for—Bill Levine (aka "Mr. Sarabeth," the name he has proudly given himself). You have pushed me to keep reaching for the impossible, and together we made it happen.

To all of our daughters, their husbands, and my grandchildren—you are my greatest fans and I always feel blessed by your presence. All of you lovingly eat everything I make, and never forget to tell me, "Bubbs, you are the best cook ever."

I am forever grateful to our team at Sarabeth's Bakery, who were always eager to taste and critique the recipes during the creative process. To Marcelo Gonzalez, our pastry chef, who is never more than a glance away when I need him—thank you so much for being there for me.

Our restaurants have a special place in my heart, and it takes dedication and expertise to make the dining experience always pleasurable. Deep appreciation goes to our New York partners: Ernie Bogen, for believing in my dream; Stewart Rosen, for carefully managing the daily operations; and Stephen Myers, for his culinary support and wisdom. Huge kudos to our Japanese partner, Ken Shimizu; senior brand manager Iho Uchida; Yuri Inoue, assistant manager of international development; and the entire team for bringing Sarabeth's to Japan. A big thank you to Mariko Kondo, pastry chef, and Kaz Tsurumi, executive chef, for their caring attention to detail. I am so grateful to our loyal and devoted distributor, Mari Miyanishi. Also, a tip of the hat to Yuka Miyanishi.

Huge gratitude goes to coauthor Genevieve Ko, for her unsurpassed patience and commitment to the project. She tirelessly stood by my side, month after month, testing each recipe until we knew we had nailed it. She effortlessly captured my spirit and style and was a joy to work with. Her gentle manner and easygoing nature moved the project along effortlessly—thank you so much.

Rick Rodgers, cookbook author and teacher, laid the groundwork for this project. I was thrilled that I could use material from our initial collaboration. I am forever grateful for all of your hard work and expertise as my coauthor of *Sarabeth's Bakery, From My Hands to Yours.*

To my graphic designer extraordinaire, Louise Fili: your magical touch is visible on every page. To Kelly Thorn, at Louise Fili Ltd, my deepest gratitude for your carefully executed design, as well as your cheerful professional approach. You did an amazing job. Brava to typesetter Liney Li—I am grateful for your meticulous work.

Thank you to photographer Quentin Bacon for another beautiful book and to Susie Theodorou, prop/food stylist, and her assistant Brett Regot, for making my food look great on the plate. Thank you all for your patience while I prepared my recipes for each photo—what a great team.

Thank you to Rizzoli's publisher Charles Miers for his insight, and to senior editor Sandy Gilbert for her guidance and dedication to the project. Thanks also go to production manager Susan Lynch, and publicist Jessica Napp. Much appreciation to Judith Sutton, the best copyeditor one could ask for. Thanks also to Deborah Weiss Geline, for a stellar proofread, and to Marilyn Flaig for a great index. Much gratitude to my agent Angela Miller. Thank you Tracey Zabar for your support.

Thank you to those who generously loaned tableware pieces and linens for the photography included in this book. Andrea Brugi: pages 220, 227, and 255 (salt and pepper dishes). Brickett Davda: pages 46 (plate) and 194 (cup). Canvas Home Store: pages I (bowl), VI (glasses, bottles, cake stand, bowl, and platter), 16 (glasses), 30 (glass), 73 (mini chopping board), 115 (plates), 118 (small plates), 247 (plate), and 276 (small dressing bowls). Daniel Smith: pages 11 (fruit bowl), 201 (plate), 259 (plate and bowl), and 276 (plate). Society Limonta: pages 12, 71, 115, 148, and 259 (linens). K. H. Würtz: pages 32 (bowl), 65, 66, and 211 (plates), and 259 (plate and bowl).